TO MARGARET

WISSENSCHAFTLICHE
ABHANDLUNGEN
NR. 3

MUSICOLOGICAL
STUDIES
NR. 3

FAUXBOURDON

AN HISTORICAL SURVEY

VOLUME I

BY / VON

ERNEST TRUMBLE

INSTITUTE OF MEDIAEVAL MUSIC
1751 WEST 9TH STREET
BROOKLYN 23, N.Y. U.S.A.

An Edition of 600 Copies
Eine auflage von 600 Exemplaren

№ 450

Printed in the Netherlands by Royal VanGorcum Ltd., Assen

INTRODUCTION

An author who devotes an entire treatise to the much-publicised subject of fauxbourdon at the present time must take especial pains to justify his undertaking. The mystery of the Old French words *faulx bourdon* has long been a popular subject among specialists. Specialised studies (often persuasively written and logically, if intrically developed) have followed one another at regular intervals exploring the origin and derivation of the style, and speculating about the meaning of the words *faulx bourdon*. Disagreement, unfortunately, is almost as common as agreement.[1] In less specialised books such as music-history and appreciation texts, the disagreements are not dwelt upon. Fauxbourdon style is usually presented there as one of the principal avenues by which parallel thirds and sixths were introduced to Western (continental) music. Due to the almost universal interest in fauxbourdon evidenced by author of textbooks, it is probably not an exaggeration to say that all students of music are at least *exposed* to the fauxbourdon idea at some time in their lives.[2] Partly for this reason, it might justly be complained that fauxbourdon is too well-known. When this happens, a populaı simplification of the musical characteristics often takes place and the musical style becomes known primarily by its reputation. Thus, in the case of fauxbourdon, a discouragingly large number of students has never analysed an authentic fauxbourdon composition and seems to conceive of it purely in abstract terms as the harmonic setting of a plain chant in parallel sixth chords. In some extreme cases, the term *fauxbourdon* has become synonymous with sixth chords, themselves.

A reflective reader, however, may have wondered, from time to time, why such an essentially monotonous style should be given so much consideration. In particular, why should some of the greatest creative artists of the early fifteenth century have been so concerned about mechanical progressions of first inversion chords? One would not expect such a wearisome harmonic device to engage the imagination of the major composers of any age for long. The logical conclusion

[1] A succinct résumé of the fauxbourdon controversy can be found in *Aux Origines du faux-bourdon*, by S. Clercx, in the *Revue de Musicologie*, XL 1957, pp. 151ff. An almost complete bibliography can be found at the end of the article *Fauxbourdon* by H. Besseler in the encyclopedia *Die Musik in Geschichte und Gegenwart*.

[2] It might be noted, that fauxbourdon is more often a subject about which one writes, than one which one reproduces in musical notation in the widely used anthologies or which one records in the various histories of music in sound. No piece in fauxbourdon can be found, for example, in the otherwise excellent *History of Music in Sound* (*HMS*); apparently, no example is to be included in the ambitious programme conducted by *Das deutsche Grammophon*, nor was any included in the earlier *Anthologie sonore*. The inclusion in the English (*Columbia*) *History of Music* of Dufay's *Conditor alme siderum* (with a rather free fauxbourdon contratenor altus) proves to be the exception.

was that the historical style must have consisted of more than unadulterated sixth chords. This inference provided the impetus for the collection of all authentic fauxbourdon compositions that could be traced through catalogues, inventories, special studies and as a result of special information provided by colleagues.[1] The resultant collection is undoubtedly not quite complete; the gathering of a perfectly complete collection would require the personal inspection of all pertinent sources in European libraries. Such a project is not possible at the present time. Our collection is nearly complete, however, and it is certainly comprehensive. [2] It came as a surprise, that this collection had not been made before. It would prove very beneficial to the state of fauxbourdon research, if these compositions could be made available in modern notation in transcription.

The compositions were written in a period bounded in the beginning by the earliest documented appearance of the term *faulx bourdon* with music sometime before 1430 through the metamorphosis of the style into four-voice *falsobordone* in the early sixteenth century. We have been able to collect 172 different fauxbourdon settings of 175 different texts, almost all of which are liturgical.[3] Of the 172 musical settings bearing an inscription *faulx bourdon*,[4] only 25 have been published in modern notation in their entirety. Another 11 are available in partial transcription, usually just the first few measures. The number of published compositions is small enough, but the interested student is further handicapped by the rather arbitrary concentration of these publications on one form: *hymns*, and on one composer: *Dufay*.

In order to determine the precise relationship between the published body of fauxbourdon compositions and the complete répertoire, we can classify the group of 175 texts according to liturgical function and compare the published compositions with the extant works. In the following enumeration, the numerical quantity of each liturgical type is followed by the number of published transcriptions in parentheses; (for this purpose, we are combining the partial and complete transcriptions.). Hymns 46 (19); Psalms 31 (1); Magnificats 20 (1); Introits 19 (0); Antiphons 14 (4); Kyries 14 (2); Kyrie litanies 3 (1); Glorias 2 (1);

[1] It is with most profound thanks, that I acknowledge a great debt to my late teacher, Manfred Bukofzer, through whose painstaking efforts I first became interested in fauxbourdon. For their continued aid and willingness to be of assistance, I wish to express my thanks to Vincent Duckles, Dragan Plamenac and François Lesure. For reading through the manuscript and for making many helpful suggestions, I wish to express my gratitude to Vincent Duckles and Luther Dittmer. Finally, I must acknowledge perhaps the greatest debt to my friend and colleague Robert J. Snow for his gracious help with liturgical questions and also for innumerable other acts of assistance, too numerous to mention.

[2] Appendix I contains an analytical index of the compositions arranged according to their functions, liturgical or extra-liturgical.

[3] The reason for the discrepancy is that Dufay set three pairs of liturgical texts to the same music. Musically, *Christe redemptor... ex patre* = *Christe redemptor... conserva*; *Deus tuorum* = *Iesu corona*; and the *Qui venit* from *Tr 92* (II) 1563 *Sanctus* = the *Qui tollis... dona nobis pacem* from *Tr 92* (II) 1564 *Agnus dei*. *Confer* Appendix I, numbers 6-7, 10 and 21; (the code and symbols used for compositions and manuscripts is explained below p. 4, footnote 2 and pp. 6ff.

[4] *Faulx bourdon* will represent the inscription and fauxbourdon the form or style of the composition in this study.

TABLE OF CONTENTS

MUSICAL ILLUSTRATIONS

TABLES

Sanctus 3 (1); Agnus dei 2 (1); Benedicamus domino 1 (0); Sequences 11 (0); Versicle and Response 1 (0); Communions 2 (1); St. Matthew Passion 1 (0); Preface 1 (0). In addition, there are four non-liturgical compositions: Motets 2 (2); Carol 1 (1); Chanson 1 (1). It can be seen immediately, that the modern transcriptions do not present a true picture of historical fauxbourdon. Not even half of the hymns, by far the best represented form, have been edited. Some of the important types, such as the Introit and the Sequence, have not been reproduced at all, while numerically inferior ones, *exempli gratia* motet, carol and chanson, have all been published. A majority of the most informative and interesting compositions, thus, is available only in manuscript form.

The various composers of fauxbourdon are hardly more judiciously represented. The composers of the 172 musical settings are represented in printed editions as follows: Anonymous 96 (6); Dufay 24 (15); N. de Merques 6 (1); Binchois 6 (5); Brasart 6 (0); Roullet 6 (0); Antonius Janue 5 (3); Johannes Lymburgia 5 (2); Benoit 2 (1); Feraguti 2 (0); Sarto 2 (0); Hermann Edelawer 2 (0); Reginald Liebert 2 (2); C. Merques 1 (0); Ray. de Lan 1 (0); Johannes Martini 1 (0); Christoferus Anthony 1 (0); Fede 1 (0); Grossin 1 (0); 'Arnulphus' 1 (0); Busnois 1 (1). Although Dufay's published compositions are numerically superior, the total output of Binchois in fauxbourdon is proportionally better represented in modern publications. The anonymous compositions are grossly underrepresented; similarly, those of composers such as Ray. de Lan, Johannes Martini, Grossin and 'Arnulphus' are not available. The modern image of fauxbourdon is thus not quite a true mirror of the past.

In addition to giving a rather incomplete picture of composers and compositions, the hitherto published transcriptions do not represent any chronological succession. With the publishing of compositions from the Trent Codices in the *Denkmäler der Tonkunst in Oesterreich*, beginning with *Jahrgang VII* in 1900, musicologists first became familiar with a few fauxbourdon, apparently selected at random from an imperfectly organised répertoire. Later, with the publishing of the Dufay hymns in volume 49 of *Das Chorwerk* in 1937, and in the same year, of the Binchois compositions by Jeanne Marix in *Les Musiciens de la cour de Bourgogne au XVe siècle*, the scope of the répertoire was widened, but the chronology became even more confused with the juxtaposition without explanation of fauxbourdon from two different sources: Bologna, Biblioteca di G. B. Martini, *Q/15* (*BL*) and Modena, Biblioteca Estense, *lat. 471* (*ModB*). As will be demonstrated later, a pronounced stylistic change had taken place in fauxbourdon by the time the later of the two manuscripts (*ModB*) was compiled. To make matters worse, the specialised studies around 1937 were based primarily on theoretical treatises, none of which had been written before the last quarter of the fifteenth century.[1]

[1] A large part of the blame for the present unsettled and confused situation in regard to fauxbourdon research and opinion can be charged to the fact that in the modern age, the problem was first approached backwards, as it were, through the theoretical treatises. The motto *Theory follows practice* seems to have been interpreted, in this instance, as *Theory mirrors practice*, rather than *Theory comes after practice*. The

The first comprehensive attempt to establish order out of chaos was made by Heinrich Besseler in his *Bourdon und Fauxbourdon* (Leipzig, 1950). Because of this work, when coupled with Besseler's other valuable studies of musical sources,[1] a study such as the present one has been made possible.[2]

The book *Bourdon und Fauxbourdon* seems to be one of those very influential works that, like Ludwig's *Repertorium organorum recentioris et motetorum vetustissimi stili*,[3] are capable of changing basic patterns of thinking. Although the title suggests a limited interest, Besseler actually deals with the functional development of the basic elements of fifteenth century music: tonality and harmony, tone colour (voices or instruments), meter and rhythm, as well as with primary fifteenth century phenomena such as fauxbourdon, cyclic mass, motet and song forms, high and low contratenores, etc. Besseler relates in his *Preface*, how he was fascinated and puzzled by the fertility of Dufay's creative imagination, and was moved to begin his study by taking the most enigmatic point, fauxbourdon, as a point of departure. This subject had become more myth than fact, according to Besseler, due to the accretion of theories and interpretations based primarily on the treatises of Guilielmus Monachus and 'Pseudo Chileston'. Besseler goes on to state that:

> In place of the two tracts which alone were the basis of that myth, the overwhelming authority of the musical sources with hundreds and thousands of compositions finally should be recognised and fully utilised for once. The principal problem was, therefore, the resolution of the fauxbourdon myth by means of a better founded total picture. The author has the impression, through comparison with the study of sources of the thirteenth and fourteenth centuries, that it is very difficult to free oneself of ingrown prejudices about an apparently well-known subject.

significance to be attached to the theoretical treatises is that they issue from a time about fifty years too late and are fragmentary and often misleading, thereby rendering them not quite suitable for independent research on this subject. In depending entirely on them, one views fauxbourdon through the wrong end of the historical telescope.

[1] Heinrich Besseler, *Studien zur Musik des Mittelalters: I. Neue Quellen des 14. und beginnenden 15. Jahrhunderts*, in the *Archiv für Musikwissenschaft*, VII 1925, pp. 167-245.

[2] We have continued the system of nomenclature adopted by H. Besseler in *Bourdon und Fauxbourdon* with certain slight additions in the present study. The oldest known preserved source for a composition is given ahead of the title, *exempli gratia BL* 55 *Patrem*, H. de Salinas. In the case of *BL*, which was compiled by two scribes, the initial N (= Nachtrag) refers to the second scribe, *exempli gratia BL* (N) 297 *Ad coenam agni*, Lymburgia. The symbols for each manuscript sources are given on p. 6ff. The number after the symbol is the consecutive number of the composition in the manuscript. In addition, if the manuscript has more than one section, its number is indicated by a Roman numeral within parentheses, *exempli gratia Tr 87* (I) 38 *Kyrie feriale*, Binchois. The number of the fascicle, if it is important, is indicated, on the other hand, by an Arabic numeral, *exempli gratia O* (2) 38 *Flos florum*, Dufay. In the special case of the manuscript *Em*, which is written partially in black and partially in white notation, the symbols (B) and (W) differentiate these sections. The significance of the divisions will be discussed in connection with each manuscript.

[3] Volume I, Part 1, Halle a/Saale 1910. A new edition of the completed work is in preparation by L. Dittmer.

> The fauxbourdon myth presented an example of how fatal the purely chance reading of extant sources could be. Whoever supports his case on single pieces of evidence without the possibility of control or evaluation, runs the risk that a new fact will soon destroy his case.[1]

This admonition is well taken. In dealing with a group of related compositions such as fauxbourdon, the problem of control is not inordinately difficult to solve. These compositions are always easily recognisable by the inscription *faulx bourdon.* This is an element of control, imposed by the composer himself, which is absolutely necessary to establish the true extent of the historical style. We have adopted this limitation in order to insure the authenticity of the compositions studied. We do not assume that a composition is *fauxbourdon* merely because it is written for two voices in parallel sixths or for three voices in parallel sixth chords. This degree of interpretation leads to a less scientific conception of fauxbourdon than is desirable. Without assuming a definition, we are willing to accept as fauxbourdon anything that the composer (or scribe) labelled as such and to reject for the time being any composition not so indicated. Historical fauxbourdon, we shall find, not only has some parallel sixth chords but other stylistic characteristics as well. Most important, it is intimately related to other interesting aspects of fifteenth century music, such as the history of puzzle canons and duet style, the evolution of the contratenor bassus with its far-reaching harmonic implications, and systemata of improvisation *supra librum* based on fixed intervallic succession formulae. Fauxbourdon also was a part of the fifteenth century trend toward choral polyphony and towards the establishment of a norm of four voices rather than three. In short, the subject of fauxbourdon is important and worthy of close study because of its inherently musical capacity for growth and change, and because the development of so many of its characteristics reflects the vast and important changes taking place in fifteenth century music in general.

For purposes of organisation, we have divided the material into several general topics. In this volume, we shall discuss the répertoire in general and the primary sources. Further volumes of this series will concern themselves with the secondary sources, the fauxbourdon contratenores, the evolution of falsobordone, improvised fauxbourdon and falsobordone, an evaluation of citations in theoretical writings concerning fauxbourdon, and the meaning of the term *faulx bourdon.*

[1] Besseler, *Bourdon und Fauxbourdon*, p. vii.

Compositions bearing the inscription *faulx bourdon* survive in some 26 manuscripts which were, as far as we can tell, actually used in performance. These sources include:

	SOURCE	SIGLA
1.	Aosta, Biblioteca del Seminario, Mus. codex.	Ao
2.	Bologna, Bibl. di G. B. Martini, Q/15.	BL
3.	Bologna, Bibl. Universitaria, MS 2216.	BU
4.	Cambrai, Bibl. municipale, MS 29 (olim 32).	Ca 29
5.	Florence, Bibl. nazionale, Magl. XIX, 112bis.	FM
6.	London, British Museum, Additional MS 5665.	Ritson
7.	London, Lambeth Palace Library, MS 438.	LP 438
8.	Milan, Bibl. del Duomo, MS 2269.	Mil 2269
9.	Modena, Bibl. Estense, lat. MS 471.	ModB
10.	Modena, Bibl. Estense, lat. MS 454/455.	ModC
11.	Munich, Bayrische Staatsbibliothek, Mus. 3232a.	Em
12.	Munich, Bayrische Staatsbibliothek, Mus, 3224.	MüL
13.	Paris, Bibl. nationale, fonds frç. 15123.	Pix
14.	Paris, Bibl. nationale, Res. Vm^7 676	Vm^7 676
15.	Prague, Strahov Monastery, MS DG IV. 47	Strahov
16.	Rome, Bibl. vat., Arch. di San Pietro, MS B 80.	SP
17.	Rome, Bibl. vat., Capella sistina, MS 15.	CS 15
18.	Trent, Castel del buon consiglio, MS 87.	Tr 87
19.	Trent, Castel del buon consiglio, Ms 92.	Tr 92
20.	Trent, Castel del buon consiglio, MS 90.	Tr 90
21.	Trent, Castel del buon consiglio, MS 88.	Tr 88
22.	Trent, Castel del buon consiglio, MS 89.	Tr 89
23.	Trent, Bibl. capitolare, MS 93.	Tr 93
24.	Venice, Bibl. Marc., MS ital., cl. IX, 145.	Ven
25.	Verona, Bibl. capitolare, MS 759.	Ver 759
26.	Verona, Bibl. capitolare, MS 761.	Ver 761

Except for the two British manuscripts,[1] these sources were all copied on the European continent in the fifteenth century or very early sixteenth century.

[1] Our coverage of British sources is somewhat deficient due to the lack of sources and to the less developed state of research into Mediaeval English music. In addition, *faburden* in Britain was ordinarily improvised directly from the plain song and was not ordinarily written down except in the case of a few tenors or *faburdens*; confer Frank H. Harrison, *Music in Medieval Britain*, 1958, p. 249.

Over 80% of the fauxbourdon compositions are concentrated in less than 50% of the manuscripts. These latter sources containing the bulk of the fauxbourdon compositions include: *BL*, *Em*, *Ao*, *Tr 87*, *Tr 92*, *Tr 90*, *FM*, *ModB*, *ModC* and *CS 15*. They were all written in northern Italy, southern Germany or, perhaps, in Austria during the seventy odd years between circa 1430 and 1500. These constitute the principal fauxbourdon manuscripts. Of the ten principal manuscripts, three seem to be primary in that they preserve comprehensive collections of fauxbourdon in organised form in very reliable readings. These primary sources include *BL*, *ModB* and *ModC*. We shall later examine the répertoire in greater detail, working outward, so to speak, from the primary sources through the remaining principal sources (which we shall call *secondary* sources) and then to the peripheral sources. Before so doing, however, we shall wish to outline the relevant theoretical sources.

Many theorists of both the fifteenth and sixteenth centuries have made mention of fauxbourdon; from among these writers, we have selected eleven which we consider representative, and which, taken together, tend to maintain a certain continuity of tradition from the late fifteenth to the early seventeenth century. We have not included the various compositions and illustrative examples from these treatises in our enumeration of fauxbourdon compositions, because these tend not to be actual fauxbourdon, *id est* they were probably not performed and may therefore not be considered true compositions in the creative sense. Thus, they are not primary sources in a study of fauxbourdon as musical compositions. These theoretical illustrations are invaluable, however, in providing corroboration for or an explanation of obscure practices which are alluded to in the practical sources. These eleven treatises include the following:

1. *A Litil Tretise*, Part IV: *The Sight of Ffaburdon* (British Museum, *Lansdowne MS 763* No. 16) by an anonymous Englishman (Pseudo Chileston), circa 1475. For references to modern reprints, see Gustave Reese, *Music in the Middle Ages*, 1940, p. 400 footnote 76.

2. *Liber de arte contrapuncti*, Liber I, Capitulum V, *De diatessaron* by Iohannes Tinctoris, Naples 1477 (printed in E. de Coussemaker, *Scriptores...*, IV, pp. 84-85).

3. *De praeceptis artis musicae*, fol. 18v: *De modis anglicorum*, fol. 26v-30v: *Regulae contrapuncti anglicorum* by Guilielmus Monachus, circa 1480 (Venetian MS from the library of Giacomo Contarini, now in the Biblioteca Marciana); (printed in E. de Coussemaker, *Scriptores...*, III, pp. 288-289 and 292-295).

4. *Musica*, Pars secunda, Capitula X & XI by Adam von Fulda, 1490 (Original Strassburg MS destroyed by fire in 1870; copy in the Biblioteca di G. B. Martini in Bologna); (printed in E. de Coussemaker, *Scriptores...*, III, pp. 253-353).

5. *Practica musica*, Liber tertius, capitula quintum & sextum by Franchini Gafori (Milan, 1496).

6. *The Art of Music*, fol. 94-112: *Faburdun* by an anonymous Scotch author or compiler (British Museum, *Additional MS 4911*), after 1558.

7. *Scintille di Musica*, by Giovan Maria Lanfranco, p. 117, (Brescia, 1533).

8. *Musurgia*, Capitulum IV by Ottomaro Luscinio (Nachtvogel) or Strassburg, p. 91 ff. (Strassburg, 1536).

9. *Compendium musices*, fol. 52^v: *De compositionis regula, et notarum sincopis et ligaturis* by Adrian Petit Coclico (Nuremberg, 1552).

10. *Istitutioni harmonice*, Libro III, Capitulo LXI by Gioseffo Zarlino (Venice, 1558).

11. *Syntagma musicum*, Tomus III: *Falso bordone*, pp. 9-11 by Michael Praetorius (Guelfenbyterium, 1619).

It has been pointed out previously that 175 texts and 172 different musical settings in fauxbourdon are to be found in the practical sources. Scarcely any of these compositions are independent, self contained works like isorhythmic motets or cyclic masses. Even though approximately half of the 172 compositions are notated entirely in fauxbourdon, they were not necessarily performed as such. Quite often, they formed part of a larger liturgical design in which the fauxbourdon was used for textural contrast. If, for example, only a single fauxbourdon antiphon had been notated, the performance of the related (monophonic) psalm was implied although that need not have been written out. In other instances, hymns were notated with only the second strophe accompanying the musical notation. This implied that at least the first, and probably all of the odd-numbered strophes, should be performed monophonically. Thus, it was quite rare to have an entire selection performed in fauxbourdon.

Half of the 172 compositions are notated either as a partial fauxbourdon,[1] or present a fauxbourdon tenor as an alternate voice, *si placet*.[2] These latter compositions are discussed more fully in the chapter devoted to the contratenores. Table 1 indicates the distribution of fauxbordon compositions in each of the 26 manuscripts.

TABLE 1. DISTRIBUTION OF FAUXBOURDON COMPOSITIONS

1.	Tr 92	29*a*	10.	Tr. 90	11	19.	Ven	2
2.	ModC	28	11.	Tr. 93	10	20.	Tr. 89	1
3.	Em	26	12.	Ver. 759	7	21.	Mil	1
4.	BL	17*b*	13.	Tr 88	5	22.	Ritson	1
5.	ModB	16*c*	14.	SP	5	23.	Pix	1
6.	CS 15	17*d*	15.	BU	3	24.	Vm^7 676	1
7.	Tr 87	14*e*	16.	LP 438	3	25.	Strahov	1
8.	Ao	13	17.	MüL	2	26.	Ver 761	1
9.	FM	11*f*	18.	Ca 29 (32)	2			

[1] In Appendix I, the compositions notated only partially in fauxbourdon are indicated by the letter *p*.
[2] In Appendix I, the fauxbourdon compositions including alternate versions are indicated as having three or four voices.

a. Actually, there are 30 *inscriptions in Tr 92*, but the fauxbourdon section of No. 1563 is the same as for No. 1564 except in the last two measures.

b. Actually, there are 19 *faulx bourdon* inscriptions in *BL*, but the music is duplicated in two examples, although the texts are different: *BL* (N) 295 = 305 and 311 = 315.

c. Actually, there are 17 *faulx bourdon* inscriptions, but *ModB* 23 = *ModB* 25.

d. There are actually only 13 *faulx bourdon* inscriptions in *CS 15* in its present state. Many of the leaves, however, were trimmed in an attempted *restoration* during the time of Innocent XIII. The inscription *A faulx bourdon*, for example, at the top of folio 265ᵛ has been half cut off. It seems desirable, therefore, to include all of the fauxbourdon hymn strophes known from other sources. This would then increase the number of fauxbourdon to 18. (There is one duplication: the cantus and tenor of No. 27, strophe 4 = the cantus and tenor of No. 22, strophe 2).

e. Actually, there are 15 *faulx bourdon* inscriptions, but *Tr 87* 67 = *Tr 87* 76.

f. Actually, there are 12 *faulx bourdon* inscriptions but *FM* 6a = *FM* 18.

The figures in Table 1 disagree to some extent with those adduced by H. Besseler.[1] and to a large extent with some of the published indices of the principal manuscripts.[1] The conflict with the figures given by Besseler may be resolved by considering the fact that he included some duets in sixths which lack the inscription *faulx bourdon*; also, he had to rely to an extent on the thematic indices of the Trent codices, which unfortunately did not indicate fauxbourdon, when it occurred in the middle of a composition, and which also occasionally indicated it where it was wanting. The extent of the discrepancies is shown in Table 2.

TABLE 2. COMPARISON OF FAUXBOURDON LISTS

Principal sources	Besseler	Indices	Actual inscriptions
BL	18	14	19
ModB	16	—	17
Tr 87	14	10	15
Tr 92	20	20	30
Em	27 (+ ?)	22	26
Ao	14	3	13
Tr 90	6 (+ 27?)	6	11
FM	10	11	12
TOTALS:	125	86	143

[1] H. Besseler, *opere citato*, p. 4.

[1] Thematic indices of the Trent Codices, 87-92 may be found in *Sechs Trienter Codices*, erste Auswahl, in the *Denkmäler der Tonkunst in Oesterreich* (*DTÖ*), Jahrgang VII, Vienna 1900 with a preface by G Adler and O. Koller. Corrections are found in *DTÖ*, Jahrgang XI, 1, Vienna 1904 and in the *Archiv für Musikwissenschaft* (*AfM*), VII 1925, p. 239 footnote 3. Indices to *BL* are found in G. de Van, *Inventory of Manuscript Bologna, Liceo Musicale* (now the Biblioteca di G. B. Martini) *Q/15* (*olim 37*), in *Musica Disciplina* (*MD*), II 1948, pp. 231-257. Indices for *ModB* are found in Pio Lodi, edidit, *Catalogo delle opere musicale... città di Modena, R. Bibl. Estense*, in the *Bollettino dell' Associazione dei Musicologi Italiani*, Serie VIII, p. 15 ff. Indices for *Em* are found in Karl Dezes, *Der Mensural Codex des Benediktiner Klosters Sancti Emmerami zu Regensburg*, in the *Zeitschrift für Musikwissenschaft* (*ZfM*), X 1927-1928, pp. 65-105. Indices for *Ao* are found in G. de Van, *A recently discovered Source of Early Fifteenth Century Polyphonic Music*, in *Musica Disciplina*, II 1948, pp. 5-74. Indices for *FM* may be found in Besseler, *opere citato*, pp. 238-240.

The primary liturgical functions of the compositions inscribed as fauxbourdon vary from manuscript to manuscript. Sources from northern Italy such as *BL*, *ModB*, *FM* and *CS15* specialise in certain types of settings. In *BL* and *CS 15*, the fauxbourdon hymn is in the majority: 13 : 6 and 14 : 4 respectively. *ModB* contains 8 fauxbourdon hymns, largely copied from *BL*, but concentrates also on the fauxbourdon antiphon, seven examples of which it includes. From among the other sources near the geographic center of creativity in northern Italy which show marked preference for fauxbourdon settings for a particular liturgical function, we may single out *Tr 87* with 5 sequences and *Ao* with 9 introits, which are either wholly or partially in fauxbourdon. German sources, such as *Em* and *Tr 90*, do not exhibit this same association of style and function to such a degree. *Em*, for example, contains a highly diversified liturgical selection, including: 7 hymns, 2 magnificats, 4 kyries, 1 sanctus, 1 benedicamus domino, 1 antiphon, 2 sequences, 1 preface, 1 communion, 1 motet, 4 introits and 1 deus in adiutorium.

The manuscripts also exhibit a certain predilection for particular composers. Dufay is the composer most often included for fauxbourdon in *BL*, *ModB*, *Tr 92* and *CS 15*, while Roullet is favoured in *Tr 87*, Janue in *FM* and Brassart in *Ao*. Table 3 shows the distribution of composers of fauxbourdon among the ten principal manuscripts (duplications within the manuscript being included):

TABLE 3. COMPOSERS OF FAUXBOURDON, DISTRIBUTION BY MANUSCRIPTS

Source	Dufay	Anonymous	Other
BL	12	0	Lymburgia 5; Feraguti 2.
ModB	13	0	Binchois 2; Fede 1; Benoit 1.
Tr 92	10	9	Merques 7; Binchois 1; Brassart 1; Liebert 2.
CS 15	9	6	Martini 1; Dufay and Anonymous 2.
Em	4	17	Edelawer 2; Roullet 2; Binchois 1.
FM	3	4	Janue 5.
Tr 87	4	5	Roullet 6.
Ao	2	1	Brassart 6; Sarto 2; Grossin 1; Binchois 1.
Tr 90*a*	0	10	Christoferus Anthony 1.
ModC	0	27	Martini 1.

a. *Tr 93*, which was copied largely from *Tr 90*, has 8 fauxbourdon in common with *Tr 90* (one, No. 881, without inscription in *Tr 90*). In addition, it contains a *Lauda sion* by Edelawer and an anonymous *Congaudent angelorum* not to be found in Codex 90.

The ten principal sources reveal fluctuating relationships between the total of all the compositions and those with a fauxbourdon inscription. Table 4, in which the sources are arranged roughly in ascending chronological order, indicates the proportion of fauxbourdon settings to the number of compositions contained in the principal sources.

TABLE 4. PROPORTION OF FAUXBOURDON IN THE MAIN SOURCES

Source	Total compositions	Total FB inscriptions	% FB inscriptions
BL	325	19	5.8
Em	276	26	9.4
Tr 92	221	30	13.6
Tr 87	198	15	7.6
Ao	197	13	6.6
ModB	131	17	12.9
FM	50	12	24.0
Tr 90	364	11	3.0
ModC	83	28	33.6
CS 15	83	16	19.3

The two best indicators of the sudden increase in the popularity of fauxbourdon around the time of its first appearance 'shortly before 1430[1]' may be found in the manuscripts *BL* and *Em*. The main body of *BL*, including as it does about two thirds of the whole, contains only 2 fauxbourdon, while the *Nachtrag* (N) contains 17 compositions inscribed as *faulx bourdon*. Similarly, the earlier part of *Em*, about half of the manuscript written in black notation, discloses only 5 fauxbourdon, whereas the later section in white notation contains a significantly larger number, 21. Fauxbourdon style obviously did not mature slowly, but became popular quickly after its first appearance.[2]

Sometime after 1450, the style disappeared rather rapidly, except from the rather specialised manuscripts *ModC* and *CS 15*. This is clearly illustrated by the six main volumes of the Trent Codices which were written between the years 1435 and 1470.[3] The volumes are not numbered in chronological order, *Tr 87* and *92* being the earliest volumes. In addition, the first section of *Tr 87* (Nos. 1-162) and the second section of *Tr 92* (Nos. 1510-1585), which utilise the same type of paper and are written by the same hand, belonged together originally, but were bound finally with other material. An inferred chronological arrangement of the volumes is shown in Table 5.

[1] Besseler, *Bourdon und Fauxbourdon*, p. 13.

[2] For further evidence militating against any slow evolution of fauxbourdon from improvisatory procedures, *confer* Besseler, *opere citato*, p. 14.

[3] For the dating of the Trent Codices, see the preface to the thematic indices in *DTÖ* Jahrgang VII. In addition, *confer* R. Wolkan, *Die Heimat der Trienter Musikhandschriften*, in the *Studien zur Musikwissenschaft*, VIII 1921, pp. 5-8.

TABLE 5. PROPORTION OF FAUXBOURDON IN THE TRENT CODICES

Source	Number	Total Compositions	Total Fauxbourdon	Percen. Fauxbourdon
Tr 87 (II)	163-198	36	2	5.6
Tr 92 (I)	1365-1509	145	25	17.2
Tr 87 (I)	1-162	162	13	8.0
Tr 92 (II)	1510-1585	76	5	6.6
Tr 90	781-1144	364	11	3.0
Tr 88	199-507	309	5	1.6
Tr 89	508-780	273	1	0.4
Tr 91	1145-1364	220	0	0.0

By the time we reach the latest codex, No. 91, we find that the fauxbourdon device is no longer used. It is also significant that *Tr 92* (I), which apparently was written in northern Italy near the central area of fauxbourdon creativity, contains by far the most fauxbourdon, whereas *Tr 87* (II), which includes compositions whose texts point to St. Ciney in Namur (Nos. 189 and 193) and is therefore quite peripheral, contains only two compositions with short fauxbourdon interludes,[1] and these are notated in a crude and uncomprehending manner.

[1] One composition, an anonymous *Gloria* No. 180, has been published in *DTÖ* Volume LXI, p. 33.

THE PRIMARY SOURCES
BL - ModB - ModC

In surveying the entire répertoire of fauxbourdon and falsobordone, one can readily observe that, far from being a static stereotype, fauxbourdon grew and changed as did other types of compositions; but, because it was a strict contrapuntal device, its growth was not often marked by pronounced changes. A seemingly slight innovation, such as the change from triple to duple meter, therefore, assumes great relative importance. In spite of the restrictions, one great change does take place, when, around the turn of the sixteenth century a four-voice chordal style (falsobordone) [1] began to appear regularly in some sources. By progressing step by step, illustrating fauxbourdon from successive manuscripts, we can see the change to falso bordone in its historical perspective to be not a revolution, but the end result of a cumulative process involving a succession of small changes. The progress of fauxbourdon towards the harmonic style consisting of note-against-note movement with a functional bass part reflects the growth of a functional harmonic style in the more comprehensive framework of all early Renaissance music. In this section, after the characteristics of the very earliest fauxbourdon compositions are analysed and catalogued, the stylistic

[1] In order to distinguish the three from the four-voice variety of fauxbourdon, modern writers have adopted the Italian translation to indicate the latter. This was not always the case, however; in the treatises of the French, Germans and Netherlanders, the French term was used ordinarily for all styles, while Italians used the Italian term in all cases. Tinctoris and Coclico wrote *fau bourdon* (Coclico also used *faul bourdon* with his examples); Adam von Fulda, *faulx bourdon*; Ottmar Luscinius, *fauxbourdon*; and Praetorius made the distinction that the Italians said *falsobordone* and the French *faulx bourdon*. The Italians Lanfranco, Zarlino and Luigi Rossi wrote *falsobordone*, but Gaffurius, an exception, wrote *faulx bourdon* in the northern manner. The anonymous British theorists of *Lansdowne MS 763* No. 16 (Pseudo Chileston) and *Additional MS 4911* (Scottish Anonymous) termed this phenomenon *faburdon* (with different terminations *-dun* or *-doun* according to the Scottish writer), while Cerone, writing in Spanish, chose *Fabordon*. The writers, consequently, tended to use their native language or the language in which they were writing their treatise and showed no indication of any interest in verbal distinctions.

The manuscripts which use this term at all fall into three orthographic groups; the first, and by far the largest, includes those sources which use the Old French spelling *faulx bourdon* almost without exception. These include: *Ca 29*, *MüL*, *Tr 87* (I), *Tr 88*, *Tr 89*, *Tr 92*, *SP*, *BL*, *ModB*, *BU* and *Ver 761*. This group also includes *Ao* with the variant *fauxbourdon* and *Tr 87* (II) with *faul bourdon*. The second group, which represents the German manuscripts *Em*, *Tr 90* and *Tr 93*, includes a variety of spellings in addition to the normal *faulx bourdon: fabordon*, *fabourdon*, *faulx wordon*, *faburdon* and *faburt(on)*. Many of these are similar to English spellings. The third group includes the Italian manuscripts *Ven*, *Ver 759*, *FM*, *CS 15*, *Mil* and *ModC* which consistently use the Italian-like *bordon* with the French *faulx* (although two hymns were *nachgetragen* in *Ver 759* by a foreign hand using the French form) Guilielmus Monachus (or the scribe who copied his treatise) used the Italo-French spelling also. None of the musical manuscrips used *falso bordone* as the canon.

evolution of fauxbourdon in the succeeding decades is traced in the central sources.

The Italian sources as a whole are very important during the fifteenth century, since the center of musical creativity was in northern Italy. Outlying courts and royal chapels as a rule either received this music later or kept their own composers who wrote their own interpretations of the popular styles. These peripheral sources, however, are of great assistance, because they sometimes notate parts that were performed extemporaneously from the central sources, and also because the central sources themselves are incomplete. In addition, the peripheral sources illustrate the surprising variety of compositional techniques that could be used in a technically circumscribed style.

BOLOGNA, BIBLIOTECA DI G. B. MARTINI, Q/15 - BL

The earliest source of authentic fauxbourdon compositions yet discovered is contained in the codex *BL*. The rational arrangement of the compositions in this manuscript is important to the understanding of the function of the style. The manuscript may be divided into three large sections:

I: Masses and Mass Movements
II: Motets
III: Hymns and Magnificats

Chronologically, the first fauxbourdon is found in the section devoted to masses, but the greatest number may be found in the part devoted to Hymns and Magnificats. The number of fauxbourdon in the respective sections is I 2, II 2 and III 15 (13 hymns and 2 magnificats in the last section).[1] The device is, from the first, typical of short compositions or movements. Another characteristic which can be established immediately is that of musical dependence. In performance, sections in fauxbourdon usually alternate with monophonic parts or with sections for three free contrapuntal voices. The first fauxbourdon in *BL*, Dufay's *Vos qui secuti*, is the last movement of a proper mass with sections for two, three and four voices.[2] The next fauxbourdon after *Vos qui secuti* is *BL* (N) 123 *Kyrie*,

[1] In the Analytical Index, the numbers of the fauxbourdon répertoire of *BL* are as follows: 2, 5, 6, 7, 8, 10, 11, 18, 21, 26, 27, 35, 46, 85, 86, 128, 132, 166 and 168. Besseler, *opere citato*, p. 21, includes *BL (N)* 320, *Magnificat*, Lymburgia as a fauxbourdon although the inscription is lacking. The tenor is very difficult to read but not impossible; measures 3, 4, 12, 15, 25, 29, 41 and 51 have unresolved 10ths, and measures 25, 31 and 35 have unresolved 5ths between treble and tenor; thus, in addition to the fact that fauxbourdon is not indicated, a strict fauxbourdon contratenor altus is impossssible.

[2] Partly because it is the first fauxbourdon in the earliest manuscript containing the term and music, Besseler believes *Vos qui secuti* to be the first fauxbourdon ever written (*opere citato*, p. 13ff.). Other reasons supporting this belief include the fact that a double *canon* is inscribed, the cadences are rather primitive with descending fourths in the tenor instead of the usual stepwise descent of that voice, dissonance is used rather freely and profusely, and the cantus and tenor are more independent than in other fauxbourdon. These reasons are quite convincing if not conclusive. No other fauxbourdon composition has so many unusual or primitive features. The compositions that Bukofzer, (*Musical Quarterly*, XXXVIII 1952, pp. 34-35) adduces as competitors for the title of the 'first fauxbourdon'

Dufay, which presents only Kyrie I and the Christe sections in fauxbourdon; the final Kyrie is set for three contrapuntal voices. Progressing further, we find fauxbourdon used for contrasting textures in the interludes in the three-voice motet *BL* (N) 168 *Supremum est mortalibus* by Dufay.

It is in the settings of the hymns and magnificats, however, that the most common method of using fauxbourdon in *BL* is found, *id est* in alternation with monophonic plain chant.[1] A more elaborate method of alternation is illustrated by *BL* (N) 304 *Ave maris stella*, Dufay. Besides the plain-chant and fauxbourdon settings, a *contra(tenor) sine faulx bourdon* is written, so the performance of the complete hymn might alternate three textures: plain chant, fauxbourdon and three contrapuntal voices. A schmatic representation of the settings, strophe by strophe, follows:

STROPHE	INCIPIT	SETTING
1	Ave maris stella...	fauxbourdon
2	Sumens illud...	plain chant
3	Solve vincla reis...	3 contrapuntal voices
4	Monstra te...	plain chant
5	Virgo singularis...	fauxbourdon
6	Vitam praesta...	plain chant
7	Sit laus deo patri...	3 contrapuntal voices

BL does not indicate which strophes are to be sung *without* (*sine*) fauxbourdon, but it does indicate that the even-numbered stanzas are to be sung in plain song. Our schema simply indicates one of the possibilities. Only the antiphon *BL 199 Regina celi*, Lymburgia and the two Magnificats *BL* (N) 319 and 324 by Lymburgia and Feraguti, respectively, use fauxbourdon continuously throughout. Fauxbourdon was most commonly used to provide a contrasting texture.

Upon turning to an analysis of the style as first encountered in *BL*, one is immediately confronted by certain obscure notational practices that must be elucidated before one can approach the music directly. It is a quite well-known fact that in a normal three-voice fauxbourdon only two voices, the cantus and tenor were notated along with an inscription using the words *faulx bourdon* in some way. Typical examples of the original notation are shown in the facsimiles from *BL* and *ModB* in *Die Musik in Geschichte und Gegenwart*.[2] Without the inscription, the fauxbourdon composition would appear to be simply a duet.

do not possess comparable qualifications. Binchois's setting of the hymn *Ut queant*, for example, is not so unusual as Bukofzer believed, for it also is found in the manuscript *Em* with the normal cantus and tenor notated (although without the inscription). This composition will be described in more detail below.

[1] Indicated, but not written out entirely in Gerber's edition of Dufay's collected hymns in *Das Chorwerk*, IL.

[2] Vol. III, pp. 1891-1894. The Postcommunio in *BL* was copied by the first scribe. For a typical entry of the second scribe, see infra.

This crucial term is to be found in the incipit of the tenor in about half of the extant examples.[1] A typical entry by the second scribe for *BL* is: *Tenor christe redemptor Au faulx bourdon*.[2] Later in the Modena manuscript, Biblioteca Estense, *lat. 471* (*ModB*), the inscription is also found in the tenor, but it is set off from the incipit, as seen in the facsimile in *Die Musik in Geschichte und Gegenwart*. In the few fauxbourdon in *ModB* with tenor text, the inscription is simply moved above the text onto the lower part of the tenor stave. In sources where the tenor commonly has a text, such as the late fifteenth century Modena manuscripts, Biblioteca Estense, *lat. 454/455* (*ModC*, Vols. I and II), the *faulx bordon* (*sic*!) is moved above the musical notation and texts into the upper margin. Other sources, less well organised than *BL*, *ModB* or *ModC*, are less consistent in their placing of the inscription. There are a few instances of the inscription being written immediately below the cantus stave, above the text.[3] The scribes of certain manuscripts used an individual wording and/or spelling such as *Tenor per faulx bourdon*,[4] *Contra in faulx bordon*,[5] or simply *fabourd(on)* at the conclusion of the tenor part.[6] Occasionally in a composition written partially in fauxbourdon, the inscription was used only over the notes intended to be so performed.[7]

In addition to the French inscription in the tenor, the cantus of the first fauxbourdon in *BL*, *Vos qui secuti*, has a supplementary Latin *canon* specifically instructing a second singer to begin at the same time as the singer of the cantus but a (perfect) fourth lower.[8] The singer of the canonic part is to read from the cantus and, except for pitch levels, he was apparently expected to mirror this voice in all

[1] One explanation for this positioning could be that there was room in the tenor part, which lacked a text before the middle of the fifteenth century, whereas the cantus did not. In later works, when the tenor as well as the cantus was provided with a full text, the inscription was moved elsewhere.

[2] A summary of the uses of the term in the manuscript sources is given by Besseler, *opere citato*, pp. 23-24. Besseler has pointed out that the use of *tenor au faulx bourdon*, rather than the more commonly supposed *tenor a faulx bourdon*, is significant. This suggests that the tenor part itself was not the *false bourdon*, but it does not necessarily prove that the contratenor was the false voice as Besseler concludes. Bukofzer pointed out in *Fauxbourdon Revisited*, in *Musical Quarterly*, XXXVIII 1952, p. 28, that the "supposedly 'first' fauxbourdon piece... has neither *a* nor *au*", but this peculiarity can be attributed to the scribe. All three of the fauxbourdon compositions copied by the first scribe, which includes the first fauxbourdon, lack *a* or *au*, but 15 of the 16 compositions copied by the second scribe use *Au* (capitalised 4 times in order further to set it apart from the incipit of the tenor). (The inscription *Tenor du faux bourdon* given by E. Ferand in *Die Improvisation in der Musik*, p. 179 and Ambros, *Geschichte der Musik*, III, p. 147, should read *Tenor Au faulx bourdon*; the majuscule *A* resembles the minuscule *d*.).

[3] Aosta, Biblioteca del Seminario, unnumbered musical codex (*Ao*).

[4] Trent codex 92 (*Tr 92*), numbers 1415, 1416, 1419, 1430, 1452, 1457, 1478, 1485 and 1508.

[5] Rome, Capella sistina, *MS 15*, numbers 2, 11, 26 and 28. For the system of numbering, see Rudolf Gerber, *Römische Hymnenzykeln des späten 15. Jahrhunderts*, in the *Archiv für Musikwissenschaft*, XII 1955, pp. 50-55.

[6] Trent codex 90 (*Tr 90*), numbers 808, 841, 872 and 876.

[7] An early example can be found in Trent codex 87 (II) 180 *Gloria*, Anonymous; published in *DTÖ* LXI, p. 33; Busnois's chanson *Terrible dame* (Paris, Bibliotheque nationale, *fonds francais 15123*, fol. 159-160) is a later example.

[8] Si trinum queras A summo tolle figuras
Et simul incipito Dyatessaron insubeundo.

respects: rhythm, text and melodic contour. The strategic importance of this composition as probably the first fauxbourdon cannot be overestimated. The lack of other explicit canons and explanations lends additional authority to these Latin instructions.

There are no other written instructions on the subject, in fact, until the theorists Tinctoris, Guilielmus Monachus, Adam von Fulda and Gaffurius spoke of fauxbourdon in the last quarter of the fifteenth century. At this late date, the fauxbourdon cantus and tenor were almost entirely parallel note against note, so that the fourth below the cantus was almost invariably the equivalent of the third above the tenor. This led the theorists to an understandable equation of the fourth below the cantus with the third above the tenor, and from thence, the idea found its way into many modern transcriptions of and writings about fauxbourdon. This supposed equivalence of intervals, plus the idea that the contratenor was an *improvised*, not a strictly canonic part, led to the modern practice of writing a fauxbourdon contratenor in a rather free manner following either the cantus at a lower fourth or the tenor at an upper third. In late fifteenth century fauxbourdon, where there was little rhythmic difference and almost continuous parallel sixths between cantus and tenor, the free or strict practice makes no appreciable difference in the contratenor part. In early fauxbourdon, however, the cantus and tenor are much more independent and the equivalence of lower fourth and upper third more often than not gives the singer (or transcriber) a choice. This is something he manifestly does not have in *Vos qui secuti*. The imposition of post-1475 ideas on pre-1450 compositions is anachronistic and should, I believe, be discontinued. In addition to the anachronism involved, an impossible problem in reading is created in terms of mensural notation. The contratenor would have to be read from *both* cantus and tenor instead of just from the cantus. This method might be successfully carried out using score notation, but this is fairly impossible in choir-book notation with the separation of parts and lack of measure lines; it would, thus, be impossible to shift one's eyes back and forth between the cantus and the tenor and keep one's place. Thus, we may deduce that the contratenor was probably read from only one part, the cantus.

In addition, many modern editors leave out some of the more profuse ornamentation in the contratenor part. In general, an effort seems to be made to quiet the contratenor part (and with it the parallel perfect fourths) in order to emphasise the imperfect intervals, *scilicet* thirds between the contratenor and the tenor, and sixths between the cantus and the tenor. This, as has been mentioned before, follows the modern concept of fauxbourdon. The ideas of the composers and performers, on the other hand, apparently seem originally to have been somewhat more austere. They emphasised parallel perfect fourths to a greater degree. Unfortunately, no pre-1450 fauxbourdon composition has yet been discovered, that was notated for didactic purposes, actually illustrating the *resolutio* of the *canon*. There are, however, three compositions where, in addition to a *faulx bourdon* inscription, a notated contratenor altus can be found in at least one of the versions of the piece.[1] These are:

1. Ut queant laxis, Binchois - *Ven* 25 and *Em* (W) 171.
2. Salve sancta parens, Binchois - *Ao* 2 and *Tr 90* 852 (*93* 1664).
3. Et exultavit, Anonymous - *FM* 39.

These compositions will be discussed later in greater detail, but suffice it to say here, that, where the cantus and tenor are independent, the notated contratenores follow the cantus and never the tenor. Because these contratenores were *composed*, we might expect them to deviate from the *rule*, but they follow the cantus in lower fourths in almost all cases. It is an academic question whether or not a performer ever did this. By all of the documented evidence, however, the fauxbourdon altus was *intended* to be added strictly by reading the cantus a fourth lower, as stipulated by the *canon* for *Vos qui secuti*.

By using this type of notation, Dufay established a direct connection between fauxbourdon and the canonic tradition of the Middle Ages. It is well-known, that canonic notation (in its broadest sense meaning *rule* or *mode of procedure*) was rather commonly used in Mediaeval and Renaissance music, and it remained so until actually the increased dissemination of music through the development of printing processes reached such a level in the sixteenth century, that such obscure and difficult notation became more of a hindrance than a challenge.[2] During the fourteenth and fifteenth centuries, when the practice of music was more limited to a smaller group of highly trained artist-composers, certain unnecessary difficulties were added to notation, perhaps so that the performer (often, also the composers) could exercise their ingenuity and exhibit their skill in solving notational problems. This well-known practice seems to have been a perfectly natural activity; although some of its extremes may be deplored, puzzles and mysteries have always been popular and remain so. This particular puzzle exhibits a double canon at first in *Vos qui secuti* but not in all the following fauxbourdon. These have only the French inscriptions. The term *faulx bourdon* is therefore a vernacular, puzzle *canon*.

The fact that the vernacular was used instead of the inevitable Latin in the *canon* stands out in startling relief. Bukofzer suggested that the supplementary Latin *canon* (*Si trinum queras*...) was used to lend dignity to the style,[3] but if dignity, to say nothing of conventionality, was desired, why was *faulx bourdon* itself not

[1] There are a few three-voice compositions in *FM*, *ModB* and in the Trent Codices that simulate the three voices of fauxbourdon but do not use the inscription. Since we have chosen to consider only those compositions so inscribed as authentic fauxbourdon, these might be termed pseudo fauxbourdon or fauxbourdon suspects. Binchois seems particularly inclined to write in this style, *confer* J. Marix, *Les Musiciens de la cour de Bourgogne au XVe siècle*, 1937, motet No. 8 (*In exitu Israel*) and Magnificats I, III and IV. We may note, furthermore, that these compositions observe intervals, other than the sixth and octave, as consonances.

[2] See the recent description by Helen Hewitt of *The two Puzzle Canons in Busnois's* Maintes femmes, in the *Journal of the American Musicological Society*, X 1957, pp. 104-110.

[3] Bukofzer, *Fauxbourdon Revisited*, in *Musical Quarterly*, XXXVIII 1952, p. 36.

translated into Latin? The composer, it is apparent, consciously went against tradition by using the vernacular in a *canon*, and, what is more, underlined that fact by expressing it also as an orthodox *canon*. The vernacular *canon* itself seems to have been merely a clever, even mischievous, idea that had occurred to Dufay. The use of unorthodox terminology makes one suspect the orthodoxy of the thing or idea to which *faulx bourdon* ultimately refers. If it related to an aspect of music (or of the liturgy) for which there had been a Latin term, this would have been used. We may therefore suspect that *faulx bourdon* refers to something outside the body of classical liturgical and musical doctrine of Dufay and his circle. That is to say, *faulx bourdon* was probably an informal name Dufay, and undoubtedly others, used to describe a musical factor that was unusual, or that might even be un- or extra-musical. If it had no place in the music theory of the time, it is logical to assume that it would have had no Latin name in that scholastic era, and no attempt was made to dignify it by translating it into Latin.

We do find vernacular languages used in extra-canonical ways in both music and painting of the fifteenth century. There is, for example, an interesting reference to the 'high favor enjoyed by punning mottos, canting arms and punning rebuses or badges' in an article concerned with the English manuscript, British Museum, *Egerton 3307* (*LoM*) by Richard L. Greene.[1] Concerning the motto 'mieulx en de cy', found on folio 15 of *LoM*, Greene says: 'Its compressed cryptic French is exactly in the fashionable style' (about 1450 in England). Its literal meaning is 'Better things from here on', while its cryptic meaning is probably 'Meaux over here', referring to the English Meaux Abbey, as opposed to the abbey of the same name in France. Another example, closer in time and place to the early use of *faulx bourdon*, can be found in the *Portrait of a Young Man* by Jan van Eyck,[2] finished on October 10, 1432 at Dijon. At the bottom of the picture is (painted) a stone tablet which is chipped and cracked in archaeological allusion to the old Gallo-Roman and Germano-Roman tombstones which still abound in France and the Rheinland. On this tablet is carved *leal souvenir* (Loyal remembrance), the only French inscription in a painting by Jan van Eyck. The portrait and motto are à propos to this analogy because, as suggested by his (allegorical) name, *Tymotheos* (of Miletus?), the man in the portrait was apparently a musician. Binchois was the leading composer at the Burgundian Court at Dijon, so that this may well represent a portrait of that composer, as has already been suggested by Panofsky.[3]

Although the identity of the subject of the portrait is of great interest, the French inscription in the painting is of more importance for us at the moment. In form, *leal souvenir* is identical with *faulx bourdon*. Both expressions are *compressed cryptic French*, which can be translated literally, but whose significance is

[1] Richard L. Greene, *Two Medieval Musical Manuscripts*, in the *Journal of the American Musicological Society*, VII 1954, pp. 16-19.

[2] Reproduced in Erwin Panofsky, *Who is Jan van Eyck's Tymotheos?*, in the *Journal of the Warburg and Courtauld Institutes*, XII, plate XXVIII (facing p. 80).

[3] *Ibidem*, pp. 87ff.

not immediately apparent. The difference is that a type of painting called *leal-souvenir* did not become popular, being imitated by other artists following Jan van Eyck. One can well imagine that the original *faulx bourdon* was not intended to found a dynasty, since the first extant example is of less than major importance, being used as a short proper chant at the end of the *Missa Sancti Iacobi*.[1]

The immediate musical purpose seems to have been to achieve what might be called in American Jazz parlance *a new sound*; contrast of vocal and instrumental textures play an important part in this St. James Mass. Both from its formal nature and its inclusion, one detects a certain lack of great seriousness, and perhaps even the presence of light-heartedness, in this apparently first use of *faulx bourdon*. In passing, one may note that Dufay did use this technique in a humerous motet (*Iuvenis qui puellam*) and that Busnois did the same thing in his chanson *Terrible dame*. Possibly, Dufay was astonished that this style became popular; judging from the rather incidental manner in which it was introduced, it is not likely that Dufay actually had expected to found a new style.

The canonic significance of fauxbourdon was already recognised by Laurence Feininger in 1937,[2] but this concept was not firmly developed until quite recently by Besseler.[3] In Feininger's classification, fauxbourdon belongs to the group of canons that provide for the accompaniment of one free voice with *tenor* function, in which two voices (at different intervals) are to be performed from one notated part. The *faulx bourdon* inscription, then, called for the extraction of an unwritten part by observing a *rule*, a certain succession of intervals with the cantus. Technically, fauxbourdon is, thus, an *interval succession canon*. Because the Latin *canon* with *Vos qui secuti* is not specific, we do not know exactly what the unnotated part was called. The reason for omitting the name is not immediately clear; Dufay wrote other *canons* in which the unnotated voice was named. Such a case is found in the composition *Gloria ad modum tubae* for four voices *BL* (N) 145, in which the unnotated voice is called a *triplum*, a name commonly applied to one of the parts in

[1] The inclusion of *faulx bourdon* in a mass which was written especially for the feast day of St. James the Greater, Apostle (July 25), or for a Church dedicated to St. James seems to be an obvious pun on *bourdon* (= traveller's staff) with which St. James, the Patron Saint of Travellers, is always represented in Christian iconography. Praetorius, for example, used *Jacobstab* as a synonym for *Pilgerstab* in his Syntagma musicum (*videlicet*, Tomus III, p. 11). In *BL*. the miniature at the beginning of the *Missa Sancti Iacobi* represents the Saint with his familiar *bourdon*. The polyphonic portion of the mass is then closed with the *communio* bearing the inscription *faulx bourdon*. There is still no explanation for what significance *faulx* might have in this connection. For further information regarding the probable origins of this mass, *confer* H. Besseler, *Das Neue in der Musik des 15. Jahrhunderts*, in the *Acta musicologica*, XXVI 1954, pp. 84-85.

[2] Laurence K. J. Feininger, *Die Frühgeschichte des Kanons*, Dissertation, Heidelberg 1937, p. 34. See also Walter Blankenburg, *Kanon C. Der Kanon in der Geschichte der abendländischen Mehrstimmigkeit*, in the encyclopedia *Die Musik in Geschichte und Gegenwart*, Volume VII.

[3] Besseler (*opere citato*, p. 14ff.) states that the central purpose of the fauxbourdon canon was to circumvent the theorist's restriction on consecutive intervals. Undoubtedly, there was a reason for the canon over and above its musical utility, yet we are not prepared to accept Besseler's explanation completely. While recognising the inner logic of this observation, we tend to view it with scepticism because it is undocumented; (*Confer* Bukofzer, *Musical Quarterly*, XXXVIII 1952, p. 35).

music for four voices. In a composition written for three voices, the third part was usually called a *contratenor* which was, stylistically speaking, a counterpart to the tenor. It was usually written in the same range and with the same clefs as the tenor and moved along with it, above and below, as needed. In a fauxbourdon composition, however, the unnotated third voice always remains above the tenor and is fashioned after the cantus, not after the tenor. Another obscure point regarding fauxbourdon notation is the fact that the inscription, which refers one to the cantus, was written not in the cantus, but in the tenor part, as long as that voice was instrumental (*id est*, without text). Another reason for this positioning of the inscription (in addition to the one suggested on p. 16, footnote 1), might be adduced from the customary association of tenor and contratenor. The singer of the contratenor would ordinarily look at the voices with clefs in lower positions for his part and would be directed from thence to the cantus part. Again, a question arises; would a performer be expected to sing the part to be improvised by virtue of the fact that the cantus has a text, or would he perform it on an instrument, as the usual contratenor of the time apparently was? It is difficult to answer this question at this time, but it does seem logical that the musician performing from a written part with text (the cantus) would sing the text. Unfortunately, there is no tangible evidence to support this inference.

Later in the course of the fifteenth century, we find the unnotated part actually called a *contra* or *contratenor* in the treatises of Guilielmus Monachus (circa 1480) and Gaffurius (*Practica musica*, 1496) but not by Tinctoris (*Liber de arte contrapuncti*, 1477) nor by Adam von Fulda (*Musica*, 1490). These latter two writers use no name at all in referring to this voice. The anonymous English writer of the section *Faburden* in British Museum, *Lansdowne MS 763* (Pseudo Chileston) refers to all parts which follow the plain chant in parallel motion as *plain songs*, not as *trebles* or *menes* (= contratenores). Most, but not all of the manuscripts with those quite rare compositions which include a third notated, fauxbourdon voice, call the improvised part a *contratenor*. Although there is no unanimity of evidence, one can justify calling this improvised part a *high contratenor*; perhaps, a complete name for this part would be *parallel contratenor altus of fauxbourdon*.

Unlike the contratenor of the so-called *ars nova* period, the parallel contratenor altus never did cross below the tenor. Because the altus duplicated the cantus, it also carried the embellished plain chant. Strictly speaking, it is incorrect to say that fauxbourdon has the ornamented plain chant only in the cantus because it actually has the ornamented plain chant doubled in the cantus and contratenor.

The fauxbourdon contratenor is unusual because it is canonic and high. By canonic, we mean that it is not notated and is improvised by *rule* from one of the other notated voices. As Besseler has pointed out,[1] the standard three-voice composition of the fifteenth century was written for cantus, contratenor *altus et bassus* and tenor. The contratenor *altus et bassus* of the early part of the fifteenth century was a voice definitely of subsidiary function in relation to the more

[1] *Opere citato*, p. 32.

important tenor voice. It moved both above and below the tenor and was used mainly to fill in the harmony. During the course of the fifteenth century, its function gradually changed until it had become a true functional bass and 'indispensible carrier of the chord'.[1] The contratenor altus of fauxbourdon moving in parallel motion with the cantus does not fit comfortably into this progressive schema of evolving harmony. Although it split off, so to speak, from the contratenor *bassus et altus*, it gravitated perversely toward the upper part of the register rather than the lower. The three voices of fauxbourdon are, in a way, similar in, schematic representation to the upper three voices of a typical four voice composition of the late fifteenth century, where the contratenor *altus et bassus*, having split in two, formed the familiar, modern display of cantus, (contratenor) altus, tenor and (contratenor) bassus.[2] In order to *progress* stylistically, fauxbourdon, involving as it did only three voices, began to develop a contratenor bassus during the fifteenth century. We should bear this in mind while examining the fauxbourdon répertoire in the following pages.

It remains to be observed that, in accordance with fifteenth-century-canonic practice, the unnotated voice was supposed to be sung exactly by *rule*. Actually, there is no more suggestion of *improvising* here than was true in extracting the triplum from the written treble part of Dufay's *Gloria ad modum tubae*, as described above. By improvisation, we mean to do something extemporaneously without preparation or forethought, and it is, thus, somewhat misleading to say that the simple transposition of a composed part already constitutes improvisation. We can express this in another way; there are many performers who can transpose music but who have great difficulty in improvising musical parts. Genuine improvisation involves the same type of creative activity, as is necessitated for written compositions, except that it expresses itself, as it were, in performance rather than in more permanent, written form. The ability to transpose music is, on the other hand, merely a technical feat, involving the creative processes to a much lesser extent. We must, thus, make a distinction betweed real *improvised* fauxbourdon, where none of the parts was written down as such, and *composed* fauxbourdon where the cantus, contratenor and tenor were fully composed, though only the cantus and tenor were notated, composed fauxbourdon is *canonic* in the broadest sense of the term but not improvisatory. Some time after the first fauxbourdon had been composed, a method did evolve by which the style could be improvised from a chant book containing only the plain song. Since this practice did involve some judgment and thought on the part of performers as regards rhythm and meter, structure of cadences, length of phrases and proper placement of words in addition to transposition, this type could fittingly be termed improvisatory. By extension, therefore, a distinction is to be made between

[1] *Ibidem.*

[2] This is perhaps the reason why the four-voice offspring of fauxbourdon, falsobordone, has been thought to have originated in the simple adding of a bass part to three-voice fauxbourdon. In analysing the fauxbourdon and falsobordone répertoires, however, we find that this metamorphosis was not quite so simple. We shall return to this question below.

improvisatory and *canonic* voices. Both are related by the fact that not all of the music is notated, but they are different in the sense that one has been composed in advance while the other evidences no such forethought. The canonic voice is derived by *rule* from a composed voice in a strictly preconceived manner. It is, thus, actually *composed* although unnotated, but, while an improvised part may be performed following definite musical precepts or using certain memorised formulae, a certain amount of musical judgment and *composition* is required extemporaneously of the performer. *Both* the improvisatory and canonic techniques were utilised in the composition and performance of fauxbourdon during various stages of its development. Unlike other composed styles that developed from improvisatory practices, (*exempli gratia*, various types of *organum*), the improvisational type of fauxbourdon developed, it would appear, from the composed variety.[1] Having made these preliminary observations concerning the notational difficulties of fauxbourdon, we may proceed with the technical analysis of the music itself.

Fauxbourdon, as a musical technique, can be defined as a contrapuntal device used primarily in the expansion or *harmonisation* of pre-existent successions of pitches of Gregorian melodies.[2] The consecutive fourths required by the *canon* allow only the octave and sixths to be used as consonances between the outer, notated voices. In this sense, fauxbourdon is a restrictive contrapuntal device that may be described as a species of invertible counterpoint at the octave, with greater limitations, however; this latter type would permit four consonances, *scilicet* unison, third, sixth and octave, whereas fauxbourdon restricts its consonances to half that number. The fauxbourdon cantus and tenor may, in fact, be inverted at the octave, but all compositions invertible at the octave are not necessarily fauxbourdon.

In spite of the fact that a fauxbourdon in performance has continuous perfect fourths between the cantus and the parallel contratenor altus, the less frequent sixths between the cantus and tenor (imperfect intervals) have received the lion's share of the publicity in modern studies. Simply by using parallel sixths between

[1] Here we must disagree with E. Ferand, who, in his article *Improvisation* in the encyclopedia *Die Musik in Geschichte und Gegenwart* states that 'the fauxbourdon compositions of Dufay, Binchois and other composers of the 'Burgundian' School (after circa 1430) show definite traces of improvisational practice in the recurring instruction 'per fauxbourdon' or 'a faulx bourdon' etc. for the unwritten middle voice that is to be added simply by improvisation to a threevoice composition in which only two outer voices are notated'.

[2] Of the fauxbourdon listed in Appendix I, only three, Dufay's motets *Iuvenis qui puellam* and *Supremus est*, and Busnois's chanson *Terrible dame* are secular compositions without liturgical functions or Gregorian cantus firmi. Almost all of the remaining compositions are taken from the liturgy and have a Gregorian cantus firmus. Except for the migrant cantus firmus in *Iste confessor*, Anonymous, and *Ave maris stella*, Anonymous, both from *Ver 759*, the cantus firmus is placed in the cantus, usually with an octave transposition, but sometimes at the higher fourth or fifth, and sometimes without transposition. Occasionally, one finds a liturgical text, such as *Tr 87* (II) 191 *Gloria*, Anonymous, which is apparently not used with a Gregorian cantus firmus for the fauxbourdon section; an opposite case is found in the non-liturgical composition (a macaronic carol) *Ritson* fol. 26^v *Te deum... O blesse God*, Anonymous, which is based on a Gregorian cantus firmus.

cantus and tenor, and parallel fourths between cantus and altus, one obtains a progression of chords in what we should call first inversion, as illustrated in *Example 1a.*

Example 1a. *Te deum harmonised by parallel thirds and sixths* [1]

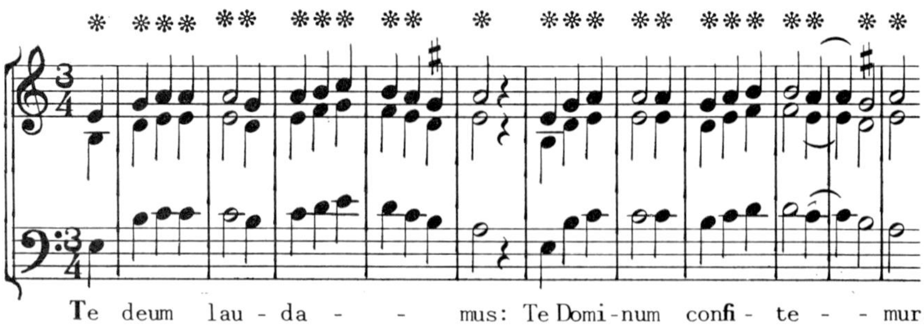

This, however, is a spurious example composed by the author. In this case, the voice parts are not encumbered by such common compositional techniques as dissonance, contrary motion and rhythmic independence of parts. Composed fauxbourdon is never quite so simple. The style of our example is approached by composed fauxbourdon only with the second half of the fifteenth century and by the improvised variety in general, but this represents an oversimplification of the earliest fauxbourdon style (*id est*, those compositions written between circa 1430 and 1440) one example of which is illustrated in *Example 1b.*

Example 1b. *BL(N)* 301 *Lucis creator* [2], *Feraguti*

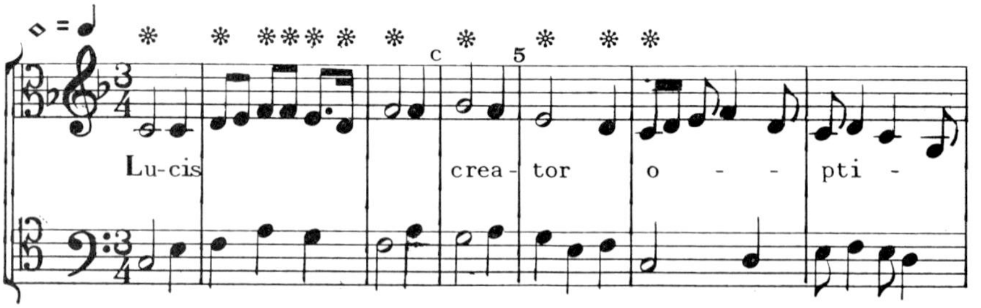

Tenor au faulx bourdon

[1] The plain chant in the cantus is marked by * in this and succeeding examples. In this case it is transposed up an octave.
[2] Plain chant transposed up a fourth. In this and in the succeeding examples, we have transcribed only the notated voices. The reader may wish to add a contratenor altus in parallel fourths beneath the cantus.

The succession of intervals of an authentic fauxbourdon cantus and tenor is not restricted to parallel sixths, the parts do not move entirely note against note, and dissonance is not absent. In addition, the textless and apparently instrumental tenor further destroys the traditional homogeneity of the imagined style. In order to establish a realistic conception of fauxbourdon, we must examine all of these structural details of authentic fauxbourdon more closely.

In the first place, concerning the subject of patterns of intervallic succession, it must be pointed out that, contrary to popular belief, the succession of the imperfect intervals (sixths between the cantus and the tenor and thirds between the contratenor and tenor) is subject to variation, whereas the succession of perfect intervals (fourths between the cantus and its parallel contratenor altus) remains constant. Here we shall concern ourselves primarily with the intervallic succession between the cantus and the tenor because these were the only notated voices. The contratenor(es) will be considered in a later chapter. The pattern of intervallic succession between the written voices varies from composer to composer as well as from composition to composition. For purposes of illustration, we have chosen fauxbourdon by two different composers, which illustrate the degree of variety possible. The following example (No. 2) by Lymburgia, for example, does not stress parallelism.

Example 2. *BL(N)* **297** *Ad coenam, Lymburgia* [1]

[1] The plain chant is a whole tone higher than in Dufay's composition based on the same cantus firmus (*confer* Gerber, *opere citato*, p. 10). Since that chant, on *f* with one flat, suggests an original chant on *c*, this version seems actually to be transposed up a fifth from *c* rather than a whole tone up from *f*.

The cantus-tenor of *Ad coenam* has the following intervallic pattern: 8 6 8 6 8 6 8 6 8 6 6 6 6 8 / 6 8 6 6 8 6 6 6 8 6 6 8 / 6 6 8 6 8 6 6 6 6 8 6 6 (5) 8 / 6 8 6 6 8 6 6 6 (10) 8 6 8 6 6 6 (5) 8.[1] Approximately, one third of the intervals are octaves, and the number of consecutive sixths fluctuates between two and three. In the first phrase, Lymburgia simply alternated sixths and octaves until the cadence. At most, he wrote four consecutive sixths. In this, he simply follows the rules formulated by such theorists of the 14th century as Iohannes de Muris.[2] As far as successions of imperfect intervals are concerned, this composition offers nothing essentially new. The cantus and tenor were obviously not written strictly in parallel sixths, but evidently the contratenor altus was, by all indications, supposed to be added in parallel perfect fourths beneath the cantus. Thus, quantitatively speaking, parallel *perfect* intervals are actually superior to imperfect ones. Ironically enough, the characteristic for which fauxbourdon is most famous, parallel sixths, turns out, upon closer examination, to be less significant than the older harmonic characteristic, parallel perfect intervals, which it had theoretically replaced.

All fauxbourdon is not so contrapuntally conceived, however; the parallelism of *imperfect* intervals is stressed in *Example 3*, Binchois's *Sancti dei omnes*.

[1] The intervals in parentheses are dissonances.

[2] Besseler, *opere citato*, p. 16 footnote 2.

Example 3. *ModB* 52 *Sancti dei omnes, Binchois*

Here, the cantus-tenor progression is 6 8 6 6 6 6 6 6 (7) 6 8 / 6 6 6 6 6 6 6 (7) 6 8 / 6 6 6 6 6 6 (5) 6 6 8 / 6 6 6 (7) 6 6 (7) 6 8. The number of consecutive sixths varies from six to seven; only about one eighth of the intervals are octaves. Actually, the flow of sixths is interrupted only by the 7-6 suspension cadences where the phrase ends. Thus, we may conclude that, even in fauxbourdon, the composer's prerogative determines whether or not the style is truly *parallel*. Thus, in comparison with the composition by Lymburgia, the fauxbourdon by Binchois is much more *parallel*, because the sixths are not punctuated too often by octaves.

Of course, the composition by Lymburgia, or any fauxbourdon for that matter can be *reduced* to parallel sixths by ignoring the rhythmic differentiation of parts, the handling of dissonances and the insertion of octaves into the successions of sixths. The result thereby obtained, however, is more an abstraction than a true composition, a product of its creator, a model for his successors.

Secondly, as far as the handling of dissonances is concerned, it may be noted that early fifteenth century composers of fauxbourdon applied dissonance structurally in two ways. One way was to add dissonance in the cantus to intensify the cadential feelings of phrase endings; otherwise, it was applied within a phrase in either the cantus or tenor to add colouration to the chant. This does not mean that all tones embellishing the chant formed dissonances; most of them, in fact, formed consonances. By nature of the very profusion of embellishments, however, some clashes were inevitable. This is especially true in the settings of chants with definite melodies, *scilicet* hymns, antiphons etc., than in compositions which exhibited tones of recitation, *scilicet* settings of the magnificat or the psalms. Occasionally, even a tone of the chant melody will form a dissonance (*confer Examples 8a* and *9*, measure 5).

Considering all fauxbourdon compositions as a whole, one observes that perhaps the two most commonly used melodic dissonances are the suspension and the échappée, examples of both of which are found at cadential points in the cantus. The échappée is a part of the stereotyped cadential decoration often erroneously called the *Landini cadence*. The échappée was as inevitable in early fauxbourdon as it was in other types of compositions of this period. In the course of the fifteenth century, it was replaced by the suspension cadence. In transition, we find both the suspension and the so-called Landini cadences used in successive phrases of such compositions as *Example 4*, N. de Merques's, *Regali ex progenie*, *Tr 92* (I) 1508.

Example 4. *Tr* **92** (*I*) **1508** *N. de Merques, Regali ex progenie*

Tenor per faulx bourdon

Both types of cadences can furthermore be observed above in *Examples 2* and *3*. The anticipation was often used as a supplementary embellishment to the suspension cadence; illustrations of this may be found in *Example 3*, Binchois's *Sancti dei omnes*, measures 4, 8 and 15.

The suspension (and sometimes the retardation) often results from syncopation in early fauxbourdon. This procedure, which is illustrated in *Examples 5* and *7*, betrays a relationship to the older technique; during the period of the so-called *ars nova*, *suspensions* occurred as the result of the syncopation of one part. *Example 5*, by Grossin, illustrates how syncopation-suspension dissonances accumulate to develop tension for the cadence. This example presents the final eight measures of *Ao* 51 Kyrie I. Measures 6, 8, 9, 11 and 12 all contain dissonances formed by syncopation. For the most part, the syncopation involves the cantus, while the tenor resolves the dissonances formed thereby. In addition, measures 6, 9 and 11 have ornamental resolutions.

Example 5. *Ao* 51 *Kyrie* [1], *Grossin*

Most of the other relatively mild, unaccented dissonant figures, such as upper and lower auxiliary tones, passing notes and cambiate, occur as integral parts of the plain chant colouration during the early phases of fauxbourdon. Actually, very few of the embellishing tones are really dissonant. Most of those found in the cantus form consonances with the tenor, but it is inevitable that a smaller or larger proportion of these will form dissonances, whereby some composers tend to introduce more dissonances, others fewer. The surprising variety of possibilities, considering the inherent limitation of this device, may be illustrated by the six early fauxbourdon hymns of Dufay.[2] Quantitatively speaking, we may note that Dufay employed the greatest number of dissonances in the composition which we have chosen to regard as his earliest fauxbourdon, *Vos qui secuti*.[3] It would appear, that immediately after this, Dufay consciously reduced the concentrations of dissonances to a considerable extent; thus, in his *Kyrie BL* (N) 123 and *Supremum est Bl* N) 168. *Examples 6a-d* present excerpts from several of Dufay's hymns illustrating the various types of dissonances one may encounter. *Example 6a*, from Dufay's *Conditor alme siderum*, *BL* (N) 293, final cadence, illustrates an unresolved fifth between the cantus and the tenor, while *Example 6b* shows an ascending cambiata in the cantus as found in measure 4 of Dufay's *Ave maris*, *BL* (N) 304. The single échappée has previously been illustrated, but in

[1] Kyrie No. 117 in the Melnicki catalogue; *confer* Appendix I No. 144.

[2] First found in *BL*; transcribed by Gerber, *Das Chorwerk*, IL, Nos. 1, 2, 15, 18a, 19 and 21. Hymn No. 6b, *loco citato*, which is not found before the later source *ModB*, and the fauxbourdon tenor of No. 7b *similiter* in *CS15*, were probably not written by Dufay.

[3] Facsimile in *Die Musik in Geschichte und Gegenwart*, *confer supra*. This composition has been transcribed into modern notation by H. Besseler in *Der Ursprung des Fauxbourdon*, in *Die Musikforschung*, I 1948, pp. 106-112 and its style is discussed in *Bourdon und Fauxbourdon*, pp. 13-14. Further transcriptions are to be found in G. Dufay, *Opera omnia*, IV 1949, and in a schematic rhythmic transcription in O. Gombosi, *Gothic Form*, in *Musica Disciplina*, IV 1950, p. 48. The pattern of intervals in the composition, which we have regarded as the earliest of the fauxbourdon pieces, is: 8 6 6 8 6 8 (7) 6 8 6 6 6 8 / 6 (5) 6 6 8 (9) 6 6 6 6 6 (5) 8 / 6 8 6 (5) 6 8 6 8 6 6 (5) 8 (9) (10) (11) (10) 6 8 / 6 6 8 6 (5) 6 6 6 6 8 (9) 8 (7) 6 8 (9) (10) (11) 8 6 8 / 8 6 6 8 6 6 6 6 (5) 8 (9) 8 (7) 6 6 8 6 6 8 6 (7) 8 (7) 6 6 6 8 (note the consecutive dissonances and the rather liberal use of the octave).

Example 6c, *Christe redempter... ex patre* measure 7, we find simultaneous échappées in two voices. The normal suspension having been illustrated previously, *Example 6d* presents a retardation or suspension resolving upwards; this excerpt is found in measure 11 of *Christe redemptor... ex patre.*

Example 6. *Handling of Dissonances in Dufay's Fauxbourdon Hymns*

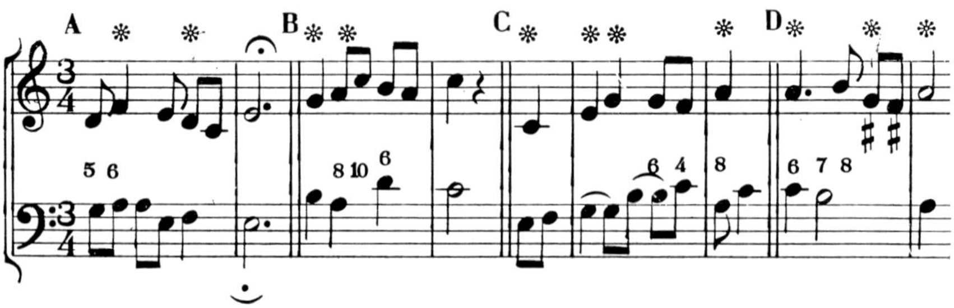

The appoggiatura is probably the rarest type of dissonant melodic figure found in fauxbourdon. It is mostly used in a relatively unaccented part of the measure and is presented in very short durational values (*semiminimae*), as in Dufay's *Exultet celum*, measures 16 and 21,[1] where it is to be found on the weak part of the third pulse, and as in Dufay's *Ad coenam*,[2] measure 9, where it is found on the second beat. There are two exceptional instances of the use of an appoggiatura on the first beat, *scilicet* in Dufay's *Deus tuorum*, measures 11-12 (*Example 8a infra*) and Ray. de Lan's *Ut queant*, *MüL* 12, measure 10 (*Example 23* in Volume II). This latter composition also illustrates the exceptional use of a lower neighbour. In measures 15, 25 and 35, the lower neighbour in the cantus is followed immediately by a suspension, producing thereby two consecutive dissonant intervals in the cadence.

Dufay's earlier fauxbourdon compositions provide the most fruitful field for the observation of dissonances. One never ceases to be amazed by Dufay's daring and technical mastery. In contrast with Dufay's effortless arabesques, the nagging use of syncopations and mechanical embellishments of composers, such as Feraguti, reveals a wooden imagination, as may be seen in *Example 7*. The very strict limitations of the fauxbourdon device tax the musical craftsmanship of the composer to the utmost. Some composers present endless chains of parallel sixths, the line of least resistance; others attempt awkward rhythmic and harmonic combinations; very few, however, are able to rise to the challenge and compose a truly interesting musical composition following the conditions of fauxbourdon.

[1] Gerber, *opere citato*, No. 18a.

[2] *Loco citato*, No. 7b.

Example 7. *BL(N)* **324** *Magnificat*[1], *Feraguti*

(Tenor Au faulx bordon, sic!)

The most commonly used, dissonant intervals are those nearest in size to the two available consonances; the fifth and seventh resolve mostly to a sixth, the seventh and ninth resolve to the octave. Exceptionally, we find more unusual intervals and resolutions. Thus, Dufay uses an eleventh in his *Deus tuorum*, measure 12 (*Example 8a*) and in his setting of the sequence *Iste sunt duae olivae* (*Example 28* in Volume II). Ray. de Lan uses a dissonant *unison* in his setting of *Ut queant laxis* (*Example 23*, measure 10, in Volume II). Although it is not actually a dissonance, the double octave in Liebert's *Sanctus*, *Tr 92* (I) 1418 is, interesting because of the technical mastery exhibited by the composer in extracating himself from the difficult position in which he has placed himself (*Example 8b*).

Occasionally, one finds unresolved dissonances, mostly tenths. Thus, *Example 2*, Lymburgia's *Ad coenam*, reveals an unresolved tenth in measure 15, as does Dufay's *Ave maris stella* (*Example 8c*), measure 21.

Example 8. *Unusual dissonant intervals in fauxbourdon*

[1] Eighth tone transposed up a fourth.

We shall have occasion to call attention to the further use of unresolved tenths in the discussion of the peripheral sources *Vm⁷ 676* and *Ritson.*

Concerning the rhythmic independence of the parts, we find that the typical independence of cantus and tenor in early fauxbourdon is illustrated by *Example 2*, Lymburgia's *Ad coenam*, and in *Examples 4-8*. *Example 3*, Binchois's *Sancti dei omnes*, on the other hand, illustrated the less independent, note-against-note style as is found in the later manuscript *ModB*. This type of writing approaches the later, more stereotyped style of fauxbourdon. As we have seen, this is not typical for the earlier compositions. If we examine the rhythmic patterns of the cantus and tenor in Dufay's early fauxbourdon hymns [1] measure by measure, we shall find that fewer than a quarter of the measures are set in note-against-note style. The contrast between the two rhythmic styles may best be illustrated by Dufay's hymn *Iste confessor*. The first phrase of this composition is written in the most pronounced note-against-note style to be found in his hymns, while the normal counter rhythms predominate in the second phrase as a welcome contrast (*Example 9*).[2]

Example 9. *BL(N)* **313** *Iste confessor*, *Dufay*

[1] *Confer* p. 29 footnote 2.

[2] Besseler, *opere citato*, p. 164 has referred to the Dufay hymns with such terms as *neuartige Akkordfolgen*, *überwiegend akkordlicher Gesamteindruck* and *der Eindruck einer Akkordkunst*. We should like to point out, that although these compositions are more chordally conceived than *Vos qui secuti*, they are not so *chordal* as later examples of fauxbourdon. This distinction is one of degree and will be elaborated upon throughout this chapter.

In contrast to the surprisingly rare chordal style found in the first phrase of *Iste confessor*, the predominant contrary and oblique motion of a large part of Dufay's *Ave maris stella* illustrates the contrapuntal behaviour of early fauxbourdon. *Example 10* presents two excerpts from this composition, measures 9-13 and 16-17.[1]

Example 10. *BL(N)* 304 *Ave maris stella, Dufay*

This type of motion is difficult to write convincingly using this restrictive device and certainly was intended. The composer was obviously trying to go against the grain and write ruggedly independent lines where the path of least resistance would have been to write unadulterated parallel sixths with octave cadences. For purposes of contrast, Dufay often alternated sections in contrary motion with short portions in parallel motion.

In addition to Dufay's compositions, two fauxbourdon by Feraguti and five by Lymburgia are represented in *BL*; none of the fauxbourdon is anonymous. Feraguti's fauxbourdon do not distinguish themselves particularly; they are characterised by an inconclusive type of rhythmic activity, as illustrated in *Example 7*. Despite the fact that the compositions are written in *tempus perfectum*, they use rhythmic patterns such as  which are usually associated with *tempus imperfectum cum prolatione maiori*. The style of Lymburgia's fauxbourdon varies from striking rhythmic homogeneity in *BL* (N) 319, a Magnificat, to opposition of parts in the manner of Dufay in *Example 2*, the hymn *Ad coenam*. It is interesting to note that the note-against-note style was apparently first used in a consistent manner in the psalmodic Magnificat before it was applied to hymn melodies. It is also significant that the Lymburgia Magnificat is the only fauxbourdon in *BL* to provide its tenor with a text.[2] By making the tenor equal to

[1] Measures 4-5 were presented in *Example 6b*, and measures 20-23 in *Example 8c, quod vide*. The entire hymn is transcribed in Gerber, *opere citato*, No. 15.

[2] The Kyrie, *BL* (N) 123 by Dufay, has a complete text in all voices, but then most Kyries do since the complete text of each section is scarcely longer than the standard textual incipit. The fauxbourdon interludes of *BL* (N) 168 *Supremum est* by Dufay have text in both voices, but the lower (undesignated) voice (a fifth lower than the cantus in pitch according to the clefs) is not the *tenor*. *Confer* Besseler, *Bourdon und Fauxbourdon*, p. 160-161.

the cantus both rhythmically and in manner of performance, Lymburgia has succeeded in associating techniques that are found later in the antiphons in *ModB*.[1] This composition has, thus, achieved an important step toward the realisation of the classical chordal and choral falsobordone style. Toward the end of the fifteenth century, the simplified style was used only for the setting of psalmodic chant in *falso-bordone*. In the fauxbourdon of Lymburgia and Feraguti, normally only 2, 3 or 4 consecutive parallel intervals (rarely, passages of 5 and 6) are found.[2]

Thus, we may conclude that composers of early fauxbourdon did not follow parallelism of the cantus and tenor too rigidly, but rather introduced an element of heterogeneity by the use of 1) variable intervallic patterns of sixths *and* octaves, 2) occasional dissonances, 3) opposing timbres with a vocal cantus and an instrumental tenor, and 4) rhythmic independence of the cantus and the tenor. It is apparent that the earliest fauxbourdon composers consciously preferred to temper the parallelism inherent in the fauxbourdon device itself by the introduction of as many polyphonic techniques as possible. It may be appropriate, therefore to designate the early style as *contrapuntal* and later fauxbourdon as *parallel*. *Examples 2* and *3* have illustrated the degrees of adaptability of fauxbourdon. One thing is clear, however: it is certainly an oversimplification to use the term fauxbourdon as a synonym for a style of writing which schematically and rigidly uses parallel sixths.

We have less knowledge about the parallel contratonor altus than about the cantus and tenor during the early period of fauxbourdon because that voice, of course, was not notated. It would appear from compositions such as *Vos qui secuti* with its Latin *canon* and from the two compositions by Binchois and the Anonymous Magnificat from *FM*, mentioned above on p. 18, that parallel fourths were maintained almost constantly between the cantus and the altus. The Anonymous Magnificat *primi toni*, *FM* 39 (fol. 52^{v}-53^{r}), illustrates this procedure. The inscription *a faulx bordon* (sic!) is found only over the contratenor parts of the *Quia fecit* and the *Sicut locutus*, which have identical musical settings.[3] The succession of intervals between the cantus and the contra(tenor) altus is: 4 4 4 4 4 4 4 3 4 4 4 4 4 4 4 4 4 4 in the first phrase. From a total of 33 intervals, all but three are fourths. Actually, the thirds in measures 4 and 13 are caused by the fact that there are tenths between the cantus and the tenor, at those points; a fourth beneath the cantus at such places would form a rather harsh dissonance. It would, thus, appear that while the altus is not a contrapuntal voice, like the cantus and the tenor, that it is occasionally modified to avoid dissonances. In comparison

[1] One can compare the instrumental tenor of Lymburgia's *Ad coenam* from *BL* in *Example 2* with the vocal tenor of Binchois's *Sancti dei omnes* from *ModB*, *Example 3*.

[2] *Confer* also Besseler's description of Lymburgia's setting of the antiphon *Regina celi letare*, *opere citato*, pp. 18-19, which is unusual both in its use of duple meter and the transposition of the (ornamented) cantus firmus up a fifth rather than an octave.

[3] Bukofzer, *Musical Quarterly*, XXXVIII 1952, p. 41 footnote 29, incorrectly attributes this inscription to a clerical error.

with this fauxbourdon section, other parts of the Magnificat present a contratenor completely free in its intervallic succession. From among the other fauxbourdon with notated contratenores alti, Binchois's setting of *Ut queant laxis* has a total of 49 fourths, one third, one fifth and one sixth between the cantus and the contratenor. It is interesting to note that all three of the oblique intervals are treated as passing dissonances and are resolved.

Further evidence for the nature of the unnotated contratenor in *BL* may be gathered from compositions with alternate contratenores *sine faulx bourdon*, which, of course, are written out. *BL* contains two such compositions, *scilicet* Dufay's *Ave maris stella* [1] and Lymburgia's *Magne dies*. These compositions provide some evidence, assuredly in a negative way, about their contratenores *with* fauxbourdon. The contratenor *sine faulx bourdon* is easily recognisable as the normal contratenor *altus et bassus*, commonly used in compositions for three voices of the early fifteenth century, in that it moves with the tenor, crossing and recrossing it. The choice of intervals between it and either the cantus or the tenor is not predetermined, as in the case of fauxbourdon, but subject only to the general harmonic principles inherent in the music of the time. The written contratenor *sine faulx bourdon* of Dufay's *Ave maris stella*, for example, forms the following succession of intervals with the cantus: 4 4 4 4 4 4 10 8 10 10 12 10 (9) 10 / 10 12 8 10 8 10 (11) 8 10......... Dufay apparently began the non-fauxbourdon contratenor in strict imitation of the fauxbourdon altus, but discontinued this procedure completely after two measures. There is no further pattern to the sequence of intervals. In some compositions, such as Dufay's *Exultet celum*,[2] *BL* (N) 310, one finds a freely composed tenor and a contratenor in addition to a fauxbourdon tenor. The intervallic succession formed between the cantus and the fauxbourdon tenor is 8 6 6 8 6 (5) 6 8 6 6 6 8 6 (5) 6 6 (5) 8 while the intervallic succession between the cantus and the non-fauxbourdon tenor is: 8 10 10 10 (9) 8 5 6 8 6 5 6 8 10 6 5 6 6 5 8......... The parallel tenths and the free use of fifths and tenths in the latter succession contrast with the rather strict adherence to sixths and octaves in the former. The association of *faulx bourdon* with a stereotyped intervallic pattern consistent with its canonic background, thus, appears to be the stylistic characteristic common to all fauxbourdon. This apparently is especially true in the case of the unnotated, canonic parts, but also describes the general tendencies of the written parts. Conversely, it becomes clear that *sine faulx bourdon* implies the obviating of these restrictions.

The non-fauxbourdon contratenores are alternate voices supplied by the composer to provide a choice in performance between stereotyped and contrapuntal contratenores. This practice of providing voices to be performed *ad libitum* is well known and has been applied in many compositional styles. It is interesting to note, that parts to be performed *si placet* were utilised from the very beginning of fauxbourdon, as evidenced in these compositions of Dufay and Lymburgia.

[1] *Das Chorwerk*, IL, No. 15.

[2] Transcribed in *Das Chorwerk*, IL, No. 18.

Summarising the evidence gained from the oldest of the principal sources *BL*, we find that the succession of the cantus and its parallel altus is firmly established for the most part, whereas that of the cantus and tenor is more variable, whereas the intervals formed with the non-fauxbourdon contratenor are quite free. It would, thus, appear that the parallel fourths between the upper voices was the original stylistic consideration of fauxbourdon, whereas the sixths and octaves formed between the cantus and the tenor were merely incidental.

MODENA, BIBLIOTECA ESTENSE, LAT. MS 471 - ModB

The change from contrapuntal to parallel fauxbourdon apparently began during the decade after 1440, some 15 years after the earliest compositions in fauxbourdon seem to have been written. Some of the most pronounced changes are exhibited in the fauxbourdon in *ModB*, chronologically the next in succession of the principal manuscripts.[1] The first fauxbourdon compositions of this codex are copies of the hymns, principally those by Dufay, from *BL*.[2] These compositions still exhibit a tendency towards the contrapuntal style. We then find a section devoted to Magnificats, from which Dufay's setting *octavi toni* is noteworthy since it involves a rather elaborate schema of the alternation of musical textures from strophe to strophe.[3]

MODB 36 MAGNIFICAT 8^{vi} TONI, DUFAY

STROPHE	INCIPIT	WRITTEN VOICES[4]	SETTING
1	Magnificat	1	Intonation (Chorus)
	Anima mea...	2^1	A faulx bourdon
2	Et exultavit...	2^2	Duo
3	Quia respexit...	3^1	3 contrapuntal voices
4	Quia fecit...	2^2	A faulx bourdon
5	Et misericordia...	2^2	Duo
6	Fecit potentiam...	3^1	3 contrapuntal voices
7	Deposuit...	2^1	A faulx bourdon
8	Esurientes...	2^2	Duo
9	Suscepti...	3^1	3 contrapuntal voices

[1] Numbers 1, 7, 8, 10, 11, 18, 21, 25, 97, 121, 122, 123, 125, 126, 129, 130 and 166 in the Analytical Index, *Appendix I*.

[2] The Feraguti and Lymburgia hymns and one Dufay fauxbourdon hymn, the almost illegible *Tibi Christe*, are omitted. The last has been replaced by an anonymous *Tibi Christe*, *ModB* (N) 14, for two voices without an inscription for fauxbourdon although that is not excluded. Feraguti's *Lucis creator* is replaced by one by Benoit (transcribed in the *Musical Quarterly*, XXVI *1940*, *p. 47*), and Lymburgia's *Ad coenam* is replaced by one by Dufay (transcribed in Gerber, *opere citato*, No. 7).

[3] The collection of Magnificats in *BL*, containing compositions primarily by Lymburgia, has been replaced completely in *ModB* by compositions of Dufay, Dunstable and Binchois. Dufay's fauxbourdon Magnificat has been published in the *Denkmäler der Tonkunst in Oesterreich*, Jahrgang VII, p. 174 and by Music Press, the *Dessoff Choir Series* No. 29. The contratenor has not been added strictly in fourths below the cantus.

[4] The voices have been designated according to the system used by Besseler, *opere citato*, tables on pp. 28, 47, 53 etc.; the superscript gives the number of voices having texts; thus, 2^1 = 2 voices, 1 with text; 2^2 = 2 voices, each with a text. Considering the voices without text to be instrumental, we would have three different kinds of *instrumentations*, *scilicet* 2^1, 2^2 and 3^1.

10	Sicut locutus...	2^1	A faulx bourdon
11	Gloria Patri...	2^2	A faulx bourdon
12	Sicut erat...	3^1	3 contrapuntal voices

We see that in addition to an increase and decrease in the number of parts and the change from a strict fauxbourdon contratenor to a more freely conceived one, that there is *en outre* an alternation of vocal and instrumental combinations. Thus, the complete Magnificat gives the kaleidoscopic effect typical of the late Middle Ages.

The consistent alternation of fauxbourdon in the vocal-textual relationships of 2^1-2^2 illustrates an important change from the original conception of fauxbourdon. In *BL*, all the tenor parts, except (N) 319 *Magnificat*, Lymburgia, were textless, suggesting instrumental performance. The isolated examples of the Magnificats by Lymburgia and Dufay provide the impetus for the preservation of this style of writing, which is then represented in the antiphons in *ModB*. The final three fauxbourdon antiphons, Nos. 52-54, include a text in both parts. In addition, almost all of these compositions evince a change to duple meter. This dual change is encountered in the manuscript by observing the order of entry of these works, as follows:

		COMPOSER	VOICES	MENSURATION[1]
36	Magnificat	Dufay	2^1, 2^2 & 3^1	O
42	Magne pater	Fede	2^1	C_3
45	Sapiente filio	Dufay	2^1	C
46	Hic vir despiciens	Dufay	2^1	C
48	Petrus apostolus	Dufay	2^1	C
52	Sancti dei omnes	Binchois	2^2	(C)
53	Da pacem	Binchois	2^2	(C)
54	Propter nimian	Dufay	2^2	C

The last three antiphons were composed in an homogeneous vocal style and the final six are in duple meter (with hemiola); in this final group, the compositions move in breves and semibreves in contrast to the movement in semibreves and minimae typical of the Dufay hymns. The settings, moreover, have become more chordal. We note, therefore, that the style exhibited in the antiphons differs from that in the fauxbourdon hymns in four particulars: 1) The mensuration is notated *alla breve*, instead of *tempus imperfectum*, 2) the number and extent of the ornaments have been diminished in the cantus and quite noticeably in the tenor, 3) the rhythmic style has approached more closely the note-against-note manner of presentation, and 4) the tenor is now also provided with a text. One of the antiphons of this style has already been cited as *Example 2*, Binchois's *Sancti dei omnes.* All of these antiphons, which were probably composed in the decade following 1440, exhibit

[1] The fauxbourdon hymns in *ModB* (*scilicet*, Nos. 1, 2, 9, 20, 21, 23, 24 and 25), are all written in *tempus perfectum* with a 2^1 arrangement of voices and text.

a simplification of composition which caused a greater equalisation and vocalisation of the notated voices. In this regard, Besseler notes that

> In order to experience their more imposing counterpoint, one should compare the early postcommunio (*Vos qui secuti*) and also the hymns from *BL* (with the antiphons in *ModB*). The counterpoint of the finely chiseled discant melody and an instrumental tenor which is quite independent rhythmically is subdued to regular chord successions (in *ModB*)... where only the cadential formulae are reminiscent of the earlier dominant position of the discant.[1]

In these compositions, the number of consecutive sixths has clearly increased. In Dufay's *Propter nimian* (*ModB*) 54, for example, there are two successions of seven sixths, one of six sixths, two of five and the remainder of four, three and two consecutive sixths as in the earlier style. Although not all of the seven antiphons follow exactly the same procedure, it can be said that most of the dissonant ornamental tones of early fauxbourdon have dropped out except for anticipations and suspensions in the cadences, a pattern which has become standardised for the future. With the increased use of the suspension cadence, the older so-called Landini melodic formula has fallen into disuse particularly in the fauxbourdon antiphons of Binchois which belong to the most chordal of all fauxbourdon written before 1450. Particularly in the fauxbourdon of Binchois, we find that the text is set essentially syllabically with short melismata reserved for the cadences, and that the plain chant in the cantus is scarcely ornamented at all. The antiphon *Magne pater* (*ModB* 42) by Fede presents few ornaments of the liturgical succession of pitches and includes many successions of five consecutive sixths between the notated voices; nevertheless, this composition is archaïc enough to provide no text for the tenor and to utilise a ternary division of the brevis. In comparison with the two fauxbourdon antiphons of Binchois, the four similar compositions of Dufay exhibit much more internal variation. *Example 11*, Dufay's setting of the antiphon *Hic vir despiciens*, presents apparently one of the first of the composer's compositions in the new duple style.

Example 11. *ModB* **46** *Hic vir despiciens, Dufay*

[1] Besseler, *opere citato*, p. 184. Rather than *parallel* fauxbourdon, Besseler terms this new style *Sing-Fauxbourdon*. He regards fauxbourdon as essentially a device for parallelism and those compositions which exhibit contrary motion, counter rhythms and non-harmonic tones as not well suited to the style; *onfer loco citato*, p. 19.

With a mensuration of *tempus imperfectum*, the tactus unit was still the semibrevis, not the brevis as in *ModB* 48, 52, 53 and 54. The tenor and cantus, although perhaps vaguely more parallel than in the hymns, still can not be held to move note against note. Dissonance is held to a minimum, but it has not yet become the exclusive property of the cadence. Upon comparison with other antiphons in *ModB* by Dufay, *exempli gratia Propter nimian* [1] and *Petrus Apostolus*,[2] the richness of the mixture of parallel and contrapuntal style can be more readily appreciated. None of Dufay's antiphons, however, achieves the degree of parallelism found in the antiphons by Binchois.[3] There does not seem to be any consistent internal stylistic *progress*, however; in a composition, where the older, so-called Landini cadence is completely absent, and consecutive sixths often number seven, as in *ModB* 45 *Sapiente filio*, older features, such as melismatic positioning of the text and the absence of a tenor text may also be found.

The visible stylistic changes in the written voices of the *ModB* fauxbourdon antiphons were undoubtedly not without effect on the unwritten contratenor. Unfortunately, we have no knowledge of the changes in this voice at this stage of development, since not a single note of a fauxbourdon contratenor was written down in *ModB* itself; one does find notated contratenores to Dufay's setting of *Petrus Apostolus* in the later manuscript *CS 15*, which will be discussed later in greater detail. It would appear that either an alteration of the cantus or the tenor effected a change in the nature of the contratenor, or stylistic changes in the contratenor necessitated compensations in the notated parts. We shall not be in a position to consider what these changes were in more definite terms until we shall have considered the changes that took place in the last part of the fifteenth century, as evidenced in the second manuscript from the Este family, *ModC*.

[1] Besseler, *Bourdon und Fauxbourdon*, p. 264. [2] Transcribed in Volume II. [3] *Confer Example 3*.

MODENA, BIBLIOTECA ESTENSE LAT. MS 454/455 - ModC

The stylistic innovations of *ModB* have been consolidated and refined in *ModC*, a double choir book from the court of Duke Hercules I of Este (1472-1505), and now preserved in the Estense Library in Modena. This collection contains probably the most instructive collection of fauxbourdon [1] springing from the last half of the fifteenth century; it is well organised, acurate and trustworthy as a copy. This is the last great collection in which two voices are notated together and are provided with an inscription *A faulx bourdon*; there are a few later sources that maintain the canonic tradition, as in such isolated instances as found in *CS 15* and *Ver 759*, but standard notational procedure becomes increasingly dominated by falsobordone style, in which all four voices, cantus, tenor, contratenores altus and bassus, are notated without the use of an inscription. Thus, the canonic element passes out of fauxbourdon.

ModC represents one musical répertoire divided between two codices, which are designated as *ModC* (I) and *ModC* (II) whenever necessary. The music is divided between two choir books so that two groups of singers might perform the alternate verses of the various psalms, magnificats and hymns contained in the répertoire. Thus, *ModC* (I) contains the odd numbered verses and *ModC* (II) the even. In addition, Volume II contains settings of the St. Matthew and St. John Passions which belong, liturgically, to the services for Palm Sunday and Good Friday, respectively. These volumes are true choir books, circa 55 × 40 cm, four times as large as *BL*.

ModC was probably compiled and written sometime after 1475.[2] In addition to the Passions, there are 81 compositions, more than three fourths of which are psalms for either two or three voices, or set in fauxbourdon. Between two larger groups of psalms, *ModC* 1-35 and 49-81, we find a smaller group of hymns *ModC* 36-43, magnificats *ModC* 44-47, and a tract *ModC* 48. The first group of

[1] Numbers 47, 48, 49, 51, 52, 53, 54, 55, 57, 58, 59, 60, 61, 62, 63, 64, 65, 66, 67, 70, 74, 75, 76, 77, 82, 87, 96 and 170 in the Analytical Index, *Appendix I*.

[2] Only two composers are named in these two manuscripts: Iohannes Brebis and Iohannes Martini. According to the court records of the Este family, published by L. F. Valdrighi, *Cappelle, concerti e musichi di Casa d'Este*, in the *Atti e memorie delle R. R. Deputtioni di Storia Patria per le Provencie Modenesi e Parmensi*, Series III, Volume II, Part 2, 1884, pp. 415-494, a certain *Fratris Ioannis bebris* (sic!), M^ri^ *Capelle domini* first appeared on the scene on the 21st of November 1472, whereas Io. Martini, *cantoris Capelle* first appeared on the 6th of April 1475. In addition, we may note that Giulio Bertoni in his *La Biblioteca Estense e la coltura Ferrarese ai tempi del Duca Ercole I (1471-1505)*, 1903, prints notices of various *Libri de canti* which had been copied at various times between 1474 (p. 47) and 1485 (p. 260). One entry could describe *ModC* except for the fact that it specifies Un libro da canto da vespero per 1a Capella de il pref. N. S. composto per Giovan Martin componitore.

psalms includes the *Ordinary* psalms, for Sundays and Week days, grouped together under the headings *Feria prima*, *Feria secunda*, *Feria tertia* etc., whereas the second group contains the psalms for Tenebrae. Twenty four out of the thirty three psalms[1] as wel as three out of four magnificats include the canon *a faulx bourdon*, but only in the odd-numbered strophes [*id est* in *ModC* (I)]. The group singing the even-numbered psalm verses from *ModC* (II) finds the inscription *a faulx bourdon* only in the St. Matthew Passion [2]; It is not clear whether the canon given at the beginning of the composition was intended to carry over into the even-numbered verses in *ModC* (II). There is no fauxbourdon inscription for any of the hymns. It appears that at this stage of development that the fauxbourdon style was used chiefly for psalmodic chants.

The style of the fauxbourdon follows the precepts of the theorists, Guilielmus Monachus, Tinctoris, Adam von Fulda, Pseudo Chileston and Gaffurius, who formulated their treatises about the time that *ModC* was compiled; we find chains of parallel sixths opening into octaves at cadences. This group of theorists was describing the contemporary (*id est* end of the fifteenth century) conception of fauxbourdon; we have been prone to accept the statements of the theorists as authoritative for the practice of fauxbourdon during its entire history, whereas they appear authoritative only for the style of composition reached in the psalms of *ModC*.

All thirty five of the ferial psalms, except for the anonymous *In exitu Israel* No. 5 for three voices, are written for two voices in exactly the same style as the Tenebrae psalms, except that they lack the *faulx bourdon* inscription. It is possible, of course, to perform these psalms with a fauxbourdon contratenor, even though such a procedure is not specifically required. Are we, therefore, expected to add a parallel contratenor altus to a duo simply because it is possible? Some editors have done this in their transcriptions, but in our opinion this is an unwarranted procedure.

The fact that the upper voice of a strict fauxbourdon is doubled in parallel fourths limits the consonances formed between the cantus and the tenor, at this time, to sixths and octaves. Thus, the simplest compositional device for fauxbourdon is to introduce chains of parallel sixths between the cantus and the tenor. By the same token, one of the simplest ways of accompanying any single voice was to add a second part in parallel sixths. There is no reason, therefore, unless further evidence in the specific case can be adduced, for assuming that a duo was not desired for its own sake (*id est* for lighter musical texture) where the faux-

[1] It might seem that there is a discrepancy here because with three psalms for each nocturn plus 5 for Lauds for Maundy Thursday, Good Friday and Holy Saturday, there would be 42 compositions instead of 33. Written instructions, however, indicate that nine of the psalms are to be repeated. Whereas most of the psalms follow contemporary usage, there are some interesting exceptions in both the ferial and tenebrae psalms.

[2] When G. Reese, *Music in the Renaissance*, 1954, p. 165, indicates that the *Turbae* of the St. John Passion are set in fauxbourdon, he apparently is referring only to the duos. Actually, none of these is inscribed *A faulx bourdon* in the manuscript itself. In the St. Matthew Passion, of the 17 phrases composed for two voices, only two are inscribed *faulx bordon* (sic!).

bourdon inscription is missing. A case in point is *Tr 88*, 394 *Advenisti desiderabilis*, Anonymous, composed in honour of an unknown bishop of Trent, possibly Georg Hack (Bishop from 1444-1465) or Johann Hinderback (Bishop from 1465-1486). Although the original text appears to have been altered slightly to make specific reference to Trent, the original composition itself had been a typically local product. The cantus and tenor move almost continuously in parallel sixths, so that there is some temptation to add a contratenor altus in fauxbourdon, as was done by the editors of *DTÖ* VII where there is no notated contratenor. In view of the fact that a constant flow of musical encomia was exacted from composers, a certain amount of music was produced rather mechanically, whereby it appears that duos would be more appropriate.

In cases where a composition is inscribed *A faulx bourdon* in one manuscript but not in another, we may logically expect the setting without the inscription to have been sung as a duo. It must be remembered that from the very beginning, fauxbourdon was closely associated with duos; as far as the notation of the two pieces was concerned, the two were identical except for the fact that one had the inscription *A faulx bourdon*; in fact, the inscription is missing so often, that one suspects that it was often omitted intentionally. It will be seen from the Analytical Index (*Appendix I*), that there are at least 37 uninscribed copies of fauxbourdon. One wonders also, whether the enigmatic *canon* was always interpreted correctly by the performers, and how often such works were performed as duos; actually, a fauxbourdon does not lose too much thereby. Since no treatise describes the correct practice of fauxbourdon until Tinctoris, Guilielmus Monachus or Gaffurius in the last quarter of the fifteenth century, performances until that time must have been more dependent upon an oral tradition, which is an inherently uncertain method of acquiring information. In any event, the addition of parallel fourths to the cantus only fulfills the purpose of adding emphasis to the upper voice and amplifying the harmony. Fauxbourdon has a fuller, richer sound than a duet, but musically is otherwise undifferentiated, being more like the increase of an additional organ stop. In a sense, the doubling in perfect intervals anticipates Dufay's compatriot, Debussy, who also used parallel fifths to add to the tone colour.

Guilielmus Monachus, the late fifteenth century theorist who gives the most comprehensive information about this style, consistently treated fauxbourdon and duet style, which he called *gymel*,[1] as a closely related pair. This may be seen, for

[1] Although this is the actual context in which Guilielmus Monachus (the only theorist to apply the name *gymel*) uses this term, we find that many mediaeval duets from English sources in thirds and sixths are referred to as *gymel*, *confer* M. Bukofzer's article *Gymel* in the encyclopedia *Die Musik in Geschichte und Gegenwart*, Volume V. It is not sufficiently understood that this is an extended modern stylistic interpretation. In this work, however, we are using the term *gymel* more in the sense imputed by Guilielmus Monachus as a structural duet formed of imperfect intervals. Since these were the common structural intervals of the time of Guilielmus Monachus, it does not necessarily follow that their use demonstrates English influence, although Guilielmus Monachus does state that this was a *style of the English*. The strict succession of sixths in a *gymel* produces a style of composition which is identical in its presentation of the cantus and the tenor in late fauxbourdon.

example, in the instructions which he gives for both the composition and improvisation *supra librum* of fauxbourdon and *gymel*:

> Here begin the rules of the counterpoint of the English which, according to the English theorists themselves, concern two procedures. The first which is common among them is called *faulx bordon*. It is sung with three voices, *scilicet* tenor, contratenor and soprano. The second method, called *gymel*, is sung with two voices, soprano and tenor...[1]
>
> The second rule is that if the *gymel* is composed upon a cantus firmus, it must observe the above-mentioned rules of *faulx bordon*, which have to do with ternary number either in semibreves or in minimae...[2]
>
> The third rule is that a contratenor bassus can be formed in both *faulx bordon* and *gymel*, and these two styles can also be sung with four voices...[3]
>
> One can also form a contratenor (bassus) in *gymel* if the consonances in *gymel* provide sixths and octaves as in the style of *faulx bordon*. It can proceed as the contratenor (bassus) of *faulx bordon* in thirds and fifths (below) with the antepenultimate being a third and fifth below, as indicated in the preceding rule...[4]

We shall have cause to return to this last statement regarding the contratenor bassus and its formula of alternating thirds and fifths below the tenor; first, however, it is necessary to digress to clarify the historical relationship between the duos and fauxbourdon in *ModC*. The fact is well known, that in its final phase fauxbourdon was a speciality of psalmodic chant [5]; the tradition of setting psalm tones for two voices in parallel sixths without the *faulx bourdon canon*, the other direct ancestor of falso bordone, is less well known.

In most cases, it would appear that this style was presented as occasion demanded and not written down, since it is so simple technically. Prior to the presentation in the last quarter of the fifteenth century of a fully developed, mature form in the codices of *ModC*, we find few notated settings of the psalms

[1] (fol. 26v) Incipiunt regule contrapuncti Anglicorum; que secundum ipsos Anglicos duobus modis fit. Primus modus, qui apud ipsos communis est, Faulxbordon appellatur. Qui Faulxbordon canitur tribus vocibus, scilicet tenore, contratenore et suprano. Secundus vero modus, Gymel appellatur, qui cum duabus vocibus canitur, scilicet suprano et tenore. (E. de Coussemaker, *Scriptores*..., III, p. 292).

[2] (fol. 28r) Secunda regula est quod si Gymel accipiatur supra cantum firmum, debet tenere regulas superius dictas in faulxbordon; hoc est numerum ternarium, sive talis numerus sit ternarius in semibrevibus sive in minimis. (*ibidem* p. 293b).

[3] (fol. 28r) Tertia regula est quod in faulx bordon potest fieri contratenor bassus, et isti duo modi cum quatuor vocibus possunt cantari (*ibidem*, p. 293b).

[4] (fol. 28v) (Quinta regula): In Gymel autem potest fieri contratenor, quod si Gymel accipiat consonantias sextas et octavas ad modum de faulx bordon, tunc contratenor de Gymel potest ire sicut contratenor de faulxbordon per tertias et quintas, vel potest assumere suam penultimam quintam bassam et suam antepenultimam tertiam bassam, sicut dictam est in precedenti regula. (*ibidem*, p. 293b-294a).

[5] Gaforius, for example, in 1496 formulated the idea that fauxbourdon in sixth chords was used in psalms (*Practica musica*, Milan, 1496, Book III Chapter 4: *De consentanea suavitate quartae*). *Confer*, furthermore, Besseler, *Die Musik des Mittelalters und der Renaissance* (*Handbuch der Musikwissenschaft*, Vol. II, edited by E. Bücken), p. 217. Bukofzer, *Geschichte*..., p. 129, has formalised these ideas also, basing his explanation of the evolution of falsobordone more on the liturgical than musical functions; notably, that at the end of the fifteenth century, *pure* fauxbourdon had specialised in Magnificats and Psalms with the result that polyphonic psalmody and fauxbourdon became identical in *ModC*; fauxbourdon, thus, came to mean monotone declamation as in psalmody and the simple note-against-note style of psalms.

set in this fashion except in the case of the moderately more difficult *Tonus peregrinus*, *vide infra*, and the more ornate settings of the Magnificat. Development of this style must have involved improvisation on a psalm tone used as a cantus firmus observing certain intervallic formulae in all voices in order to provide an organisational system that would regulate all voices in an acceptable and euphonious manner.

In written form, the tradition of *harmonising* psalm tones in simple duet style can be traced back to the second quarter of the fifteenth century. It appears, thus, to have been developed at approximately the same time as fauxbourdon itself. We find, for example, eight psalm-tone formulae in white notation without text in the manuscript *Em* from the monastery of St. Emmeram at Ratisbon.[1] The almost unornamented psalm tone is presented in the (undesignated) cantus untransposed, while a *tenor* is written in unisons and thirds *above* it. Unless the cantus was transposed an octave higher, the tenor obviously lay unnaturally above it. If the cantus (firmus) is transposed up an octave,[2] it will, of course, produce the normal sixths and octaves with the tenor, as shown in *Example 12*.

Example 12. *Em* **184** *Psalm tone formula* **2**[i] *Toni*

This proposed method of performance preserves the usual relationship of cantus and tenor, and produces a method of setting the psalm tone, which is found again in later sources, *scilicet Tr 90*, Montecassino, Bibl. Abbaz. MS 871 N (MC), *ModC* and *Ver 759*. In the Neapolitan MS, *MC*, from the second half of the fifteenth century, the five (anonymous) settings of the Sunday Vesper psalms, *scilicet Dixit Dominus* (presented as *Example 13*), *Confitebor tibi*, *Beatus vir*, *Laudate pueri* and *Laudate Dominus* (folios 17-24), are written for cantus and tenor in sixths with octaves at the cadences.

[1] *Confer* Dezés, *opere citato*, index numbers 182-189. There are two formulae for the first tone, with finales on *g* and *d*, and one for each of the others except for the eighth and the tonus peregrinus, both of which are missing altogether. None of the formulae has a clef indicated except the one in the second tone, which we have adduced as *Example 12*; the clef, however, becomes selfevident from the formula, the tone of which is indicated in each case.

[2] Guilielmus Monachus describes the practice of transposing the *counterpoint*, not the cantus firmus, an octave higher, (Coussemaker, *Scriptores*..., III, p. 289; facsimile in *Die Musik in Geschichte und Gegenwart*, Volume V, facing columns 1057-1058).

Example 13. *Dixit Dominus, Anonymous MC folios 17v-18r*

This style, like that of the formulae in *Em*, is mechanically the same as fauxbourdon, but the essential *canon* is missing. The cantus firmus is contained in the upper part, but, unlike the formulae of *Em*, texts are underlaid for all verses.

The same procedure is followed in the first section of *ModC*, which contains ferial vesper psalms. The only difference is that these duos are enhanced in performance by the alternation of the verses between two choirs. In the later Verona manuscript, *Ver 759*, only three of the thirteen psalms utilise a cantus-tenor duo in sixths; the remainder of the psalms either calls expressly for *faulx bordon* or presents three or four notated voices.

Ver 759 will be discussed in more detail in the section devoted to those peripheral sources containing fauxbourdon, but the Neapolitan manuscript *MC* must be examined at this time because, although it does not contain any composition inscribed *A faulx bourdon*,[1] it does include an unique setting of *In exitu*

[1] Dufay's *Christe redemptor... ex patre*, which is indicated for performance *A faulx bourdon* in *BL* and in other manuscripts, lacks the *canon* in *MC*.

Israel for four voices in falso-bordone style by the Spanish composer Pedro Oriola,[1] as transcribed in *Example 14* on p. 48. This composition clearly illustrates the statement by Guilielmus Monachus that gymel and fauxbourdon could be sung with four voices (*confer supra* p. 43-44).

As in the case of the psalms for two voices, the cantus firmus (in this case the *Tonus peregrinus*) is contained in the upper voice in *Example 14*, and the cantus and tenor observe only the consonances of the sixth and octave; in addition, however, a contratenor proceeds beneath the tenor "in thirds and fifths, with the antepenultimate and penultimate being a third and a fifth" respectively, as Guilielmus Monachus prescribed (*confer supra* p. 44). The contratenor altus, whose main function is to augment the harmony, is not added in parallel fourths beneath the cantus but maintains, rather, thirds and fourths above the tenor, crossing that voice on occasion. This setting appears to be the earliest completely notated falsobordone that has as yet been discovered.

Guilielmus Monachus (circa 1480) describes the method used by Oriola in constructing a four-voice composition from a cantus and tenor in sixths and octaves. It is of little consequence, whether the sixths and octaves had been the outer voices of a fauxbourdon or the parts of a duo; it is only necessary, as far as Guilielmus Monachus is concerned, that there be structural use of sixths and octaves.

> If the soprano of faulxbordon forms sixths and octaves (with the tenor), make a contratenor bassus progressing below the tenor in thirds and fifths; the penultimate is always to be a fifth below the tenor, which will form a tenth with the soprano, and the antepenultimate will be a third below. It will, thus, alternate between lower fifths and thirds, the first and last notes forming a lower octave or an unison.
>
> The contra(tenor) altus of this fauxbordon takes the fourth above the tenor as its penultimate and the third above as its antepenultimate. Proceed in this fashion above the tenor.[2]

[1] There is some doubt about the proper dates of this composer. He is mentioned as a singer in the chapel of Alfonso of Arragón, King of Naples (1437-1458), in 1444 (Oriolla) and 1455 (Orilia); see Camillo Minieri Riccio, *Alcuni fatti di Alfonso I. di Aragona...*, in the *Arch. stor. per le prov. napoletane*, *Anno VI*, (1881). Anglés, however, in his *La Música en la corte de los reyos católicos* I, 1941, quotes a passage according to which a certain Pedro Oriuela scrit per capellan cantor de la capella de Sa Alteza por mandato de Su Alteza (el rey Fernando el Católico) per muerte de Diego Alderete. This last personage, according to Anglés, had been appointed a singer at the court of Ferdinand I in Carceres on the 16th of April 1479 and had died soon thereafter. If Oriola was appointed to fill the vacancy caused by Alderete's demise, it is doubtful that he had been a member of the chapel previously, although it is possible that he was merely advanced in rank. This, then, is somewhat difficult to reconcile with the information gathered by Minieri Riccio, however, according to which Oriola had been a member of the chapel since at least 1444 (which would have made him quite advanced in years in 1479 for the position). It is certainly clear, however, that there was a composer by the name of Oriola, who was active during the second half of the fifteenth century.

[2] (fol. 28^r) Quarta regula est quod faulx bordon faciat supranam suum per sextas et octavas, facies contratenorem bassum descendentem subtus tenorem per quintas et tertias bassas; sed quod semper penultima sit quinta bassa subtus tenorem, que erit decima cum suprano, et antepenultima erit tertia bassa; et sic iterando per quintas bassas et tertias bassas, ita quod prima nota sit octava bassa vel unisonus, et ultima sit octava bassa vel unisonus. Contra vero altus istius Faulxbordon accipiet suam penultimam quartam supra tenorem et suam antepenultimam tertiam supra tenorem, et sic itinerando supra tenorem (Coussemaker, *Scriptores...*, III, p. 293b).

Example 14. *MC 7 In exitu Israel, Oriola* [1] *MC folio* 4, *p.* 253

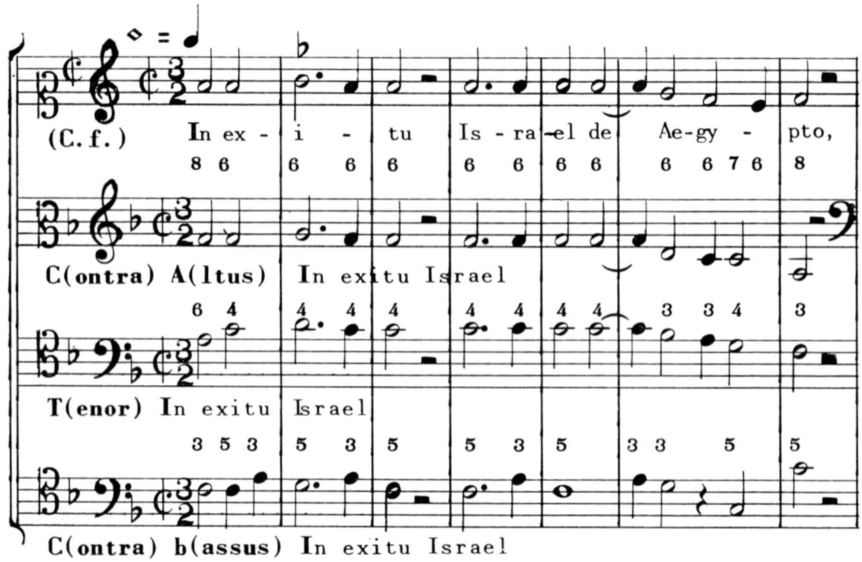

[1] The numbers under the soprano part refer to the intervals formed between the soprano and the tenor; those under the altus *similiter* between the altus and the tenor, and those beneath the tenor part refer to the intervals formed between that voice and the bassus. This procedure will be followed in all similar examples below.

We present below a schematic diagram of the intervallic succession of the first phrase of Oriola's *In exitu*, which gives a practical illustration of the formulae described by Guilielmus Monachus.

Cantus Tenor	8	6	6	6	6	/	6	6	6	6	6	6	(7)6	8
Altus Tenor	6	4	4	4	4	/	4	4	4	4	3	3	4	3
Tenor		/\									\	/		
Bassus	3	5 3	5	3	5	/	5	3	5	3	3		5	+5

The contratenor bassus adheres almost slavishly to the alternation of thirds and fifths except for the two consecutive thirds in measure 6. Apparently, Oriola wrote two consecutive thirds at this point to simplify the passage to the fifth in the penultimate of the phrase; this actually results in the dominant-tonic cadence of 18th-19th century harmony. Again, one might note a deviation in the final note in the contratenor bassus, which jumps up to the fifth above the tenor as if it were a contratenor *altus et bassus*,[1] instead of forming an octave with the tenor, or even an unison.

Oriola's contratenor altus does not correspond quite so well to Guilielmus Monachus's formula as the bassus. It is true that most of the intervals form fourths or thirds, as specified, but these intervals do not alternate with each other in any regular manner. The altus is not quite the same as the parallel altus of fauxbourdon; such an altus was intended to be the sole contratenor and performed together with only the cantus and the tenor, while the altus in this instance tends only to amplify the harmony and is used in conjunction with the bassus. In other words, the parallel altus has its place in three-voice fauxbourdon, while the amplifying altus is used in four-voice fauxbourdon, which is often called falsobordone in the scientific literature. We shall return later to fauxbourdon and falsobordone compositions that utilise the formula which alternates fourths and thirds above the tenor with a little more consistency than in Oriola's *In exitu*.

These formulae represent additional solutions for the intervallic succession *canon* of *faulx bourdon*. The earliest solution which we have adduced, *scilicet* the succession of parallel fourths beneath the cantus, has been known in the scientific literature for quite some time, but the practical use of the additional formulae has not been applied in the transcription and realisation of the musical compositions in these sources. Paradoxically, there are many more notated examples of the contratenor bassus and amplifying altus than there are of the more familiar parallel altus. We, thus, find that the scientific writings are replete with oversimplifications of the fauxbourdon contratenor as well as of the stylistic characteristics of the written voices.

[1] A more complete discussion of the historical significance of this type cadence is included in Besseler, *Bourdon und Fauxbourdon*, pp. 33-34. Actually, Guilielmus Monachus uses this cadence in his musical examples although he does not describe it in his text. *Confer* the transcription in Bukofzer, *Musical Quarterly*, XXXVIII 1952, p. 44, measure 9.

Guilielmus Monachus's description of the contratenor bassus with its amplifying altus to be added by *rule* to the tenor of fauxbourdon or gymel in sixths clearly reveals the canonic ancestry of these voices and establishes their relationship to the earlier parallel altus. The bassus and the amplifying altus are genuine fauxbourdon contratenores; perhaps, they developed from a tradition in which alternate contratenores were provided for fauxbourdon.

This system of fixed intervallic succession though canonic in origin, was emminently suited to improvisation *supra librum*. If we provide a suitable chant, the cantus could sing sixths above the Gregorian tenor, the bassus could alternate thirds and fifths beneath the tenor, and the amplifying altus could synchronise its thirds and fourths above the tenor with the bassus. In the case of many chants, the result produces a very satisfactory *harmonisation* in, what we should call, root positions (as we shall illustrate below). The results are not quite so satisfactory if the chant, for example, does not have the usual stepwise descending cadence at the ends of phrases. It, thus, appears, that further systematisation was required to produce a satisfactory *harmonisation* from a notated, untransposed psalm tone to guarantee the euphony of the presentation. Fortunately, many of the fully notated falsobordone psalms show their very close relationship to the mechanical model which may be presented *supra librum*; such settings, as Oriola's *In exitu*, provide us with information about the improvised style, which we could not otherwise obtain. Before investigating the use of intervallic succession formulae further, however, we must inspect other psalm settings.

In exitu was set polyphonically quite often by composers other than Oriola. *ModB* and *FM*, for example, each contains a separate version of a setting by Binchois; *ModB* arranges the composition for three voices and a fauxbourdon-like contratenor altus, whereas *FM* presents only a cantus-tenor duo without either an altus or a *faulx bourdon* canon.[1]

In exitu is set polyphonically in three different ways in *Tr 90*. Two of the compositions, Nos. 1059 and 1096, exhibit parallel sixths in the manner of *faulx bourdon*, but only No. 1096 includes the *canon*. The third setting, No. 1095, utilises fauxbourdon and three free voices. Comparing all of the settings with each other, we see in a small way the organisational idea underlining the later manuscript *ModC*, which similarly contains duos, fauxbourdon and three-voice settings of psalms. By way of contrast, in *ModC* itself, *In exitu* is composed for three free voices. In this setting, the cantus and tenor rely primarily on sixths, but they also inject many thirds and fifths. The bassus does not alternate thirds and fifths, as in the formula in Oriola's setting of *In exitu*. In fact, as concerns the succession of intervals, this is the least restricted of all the psalm settings in *ModC*. In further enumerating compositions for two voices in sixths without the fauxbourdon

[1] Transcribed (from *ModB*) in J. Marix, *Les Musiciens de la cour de Bourgogne au XVe siècle*, 1937, as Binchois's motet No. 8. Besseler, in *Studien zur Musik des Mittelalters*: I, in the *Archiv für Musikwissenschaft*, VII 1925, pp. 238-239, in the index of incipits in *FM*, notes a duo with a third voice to be added *a faulx bourdon*. Unfortunately, there is no such *canon* present.

canon, we should also take note of the numerous introits contained in *Tr 90* [1] as well as *BL* (N) 320 *Magnificat*, Lymburgia and *Ao* 168 *Magnificat*, Anonymous. It will be noticed that these liturgical types are all closely related to psalmody.

On the basis of this evidence, one may conclude that the tradition of performing chants based on recitation formulae in simple parallel sixths was as old as that of fauxbourdon in general, both coming into vogue around 1430. *ModC* has, therefore, merely incorporated these duets with the fauxbourdon into one collection toward the end of the fifteenth century. From this time on, it would appear that the two styles merge and result in what is called *falsobordone* in the scientific literature. By closer examination of the compositions in *ModC*, we can follow the various stages in the metamorphosis to falsobordone.

The thirty three Tenebrae psalms are most instructive in this regard. These settings include verses for two voices in sixths (which Guilielmus Monachus would have termed *gymel*) that reflect the line of development previously traced, there is fauxbourdon and, finally, there are three-voice settings illustrating incipient falsobordone style. The table below presents a summary of the compositional techniques utilised in the Tenebrae psalms according to the two volumes of *ModC*.

	PSALM	PSALM NO.	SETTING [2] I	II	LITURGICAL FUNCTION
49.	Salvum me fac	68	3	3	Fer. 5 p^{mo} noct.
50.	Deus in adiutorium	89	3	3	
51.	In te, Domine, speravi	70	3	3	
52.	Deus, iudicium	71	Fb	2	In 2° nocturno
53.	Quam bonus	72	3 & Fb	3 & 2	
54.	Ut quid	73	3 & Fb	3	
55.	Confitebimur	74	Fb	2	In 3° nocturno
56.	Notus in Iudea	75	Fb	3	
57.	Voce mea... et	76	Fb	2	
58.	Miserere mei	50	3	3	In laudibus
59.	Domine, refugium	89	3 & Fb	3	
60.	Deus, Deus meus, ad te	62	3	2	
61.	Cantemus dominus	Canticle	Fb	2	
62.	Laudate Dominus de celis	148	3	3	
63.	Benedictus dom... Israël	Canticle	Fb	2	
64.	Quare fremuerunt	2	3	3	F. 6° in 1° noct.
65.	Deus, Deus meus, respice	21	2	2	
66.	Dominus illuminatio	26	Fb	3	
67.	Domine, ne in fuore	37	3 & Fb	3	In 2° nocturno

[1] Numbers 796, 802, 809, 814, 831, 832, 835, 841, 844 (and also a Kyrie, No. 884).
[2] Text in all notated voices.

68.	Expectans	39	Fb	2	
69.	Deus, in nomine	53	Fb	2	
70.	Eripe me de inimicis	58	Fb	3	In 3° nocturno
71.	Nomine, Deus salutis	87	3 & Fb	3	
72.	Deus ultionum	93	Fb	3	
73.	Domine, exaudi... auribus	142	Fb	2	In laudibus
74.	Domini audivi	Canticle	Fb	2	
75.	Dum invocarem	4	Fb	2	Sabbato 1° noct.
76.	Domine, quis habitabit	14	Fb	2	
77.	Conserva me, Domine	15	Fb	2	
78.	Domini est terra	23	Fb	2	
79.	Exaltabo te, Domine	29	Fb	2	
80.	Iudica me	42	Fb	2	In laudibus
81.	Ego dixi	Canticle	2	2	

Six psalms (Nos. 49, 50, 51, 58, 62 and 64) are written entirely for three voices and two are simply duos without fauxbourdon (Nos. 65, and 81). Nine psalms (Nos. 53, 54, 56, 59, 66, 67, 70, 71 and 72) combine verses in fauxbourdon with verses for three written voices, and one (No. 60) combines verses for two voices without fauxbourdon (in Chorus II) with verses for three written voices (in Chorus I). There is some doubt about the intended mode of performance of the remaining fifteen psalms. If one assumes that the second choir continued the fauxbourdon style of the first choir in the realisation of their music, even though their verses are not specifically labelled *A faulx bourdon*, then, we should have fifteen psalms entirely in fauxbourdon (Nos. 52, 55, 57, 61, 63, 68, 69, 73, 74, 75, 76, 77, 78, 79 and 80). The contrast between fauxbourdon in the first chorus and duos in the second has much to favour the reduced setting of the alternate verses as sung by the second chorus.

The duos and the fauxbourdon settings all move essentially in parallel sixths, while the three-voice compositions apply different formulae to a greater or lesser extent. Formulae are applied increasingly as one advances through the source. The freest conceived setting appears to be the fifth composition, *In exitu*, whereas by the time one has reached the sixty fourth of these psalms, the cantus and tenor move almost exclusively in sixths (with octave cadences) and the bassus alternates thirds and fifths beneath the tenor, as has been exemplified in Oriola's setting of *In exitu* (*Example 14*). Beginning with No. 73, *Domine, exaudi*, and continuing on to the last psalm setting, we find that the third voice is omitted altogether and the cantus and tenor are written entirely in sixths (with octave cadences) with the fauxbourdon *canon*. If the order of entry of the composition into *ModC* also represents the succession of composition of the individual piece, then it would appear that the composer(s) of the multiversed psalms apparently wearied of their task and fell back more and more upon formulae.

The differences among the psalm tones themselves seem to have played a rôle in choosing the type of setting for a particular psalm. Tones 4, 5 and 7 are composed only for fauxbourdon or duo; only psalm tones 1, 2 (transposed) and 8 are provided with an additional bassus.[1]

Example 15, a verse from *Notus in Iudea* (Psalm 75), is illustrative of both the duet style in sixths and the setting in fauxbourdon. This one excerpt will suffice for both, since the only difference in the compositional technique between a duo and fauxbourdon is in the inscription.

Example 15. *ModC* 56, *Notus in Iudea*, *Anonymous* (*Transposed 2nd Tone*)

faulx bordon

faulx bordon **Tenor:**

One will note the progression of sixths in note-against-note style with the cantus firmus in the top voice, which was typical of late fauxbourdon. At the ends of phrases, we find almost invariably 7-6 suspensions leading to an octave as final cadence. This pattern is used throughout *ModC* where two written voices are involved. For the incipient falsobordone style, a bassus observing the intervallic succession formula of fauxbourdon is added to this basic structure. *Example 16* illustrates this addition.

[1] Since the Tenebrae psalms do not make use of the third and sixth tones, these are, of course, not set polyphonically.

Example 16. *ModC 72, Deus ultionem, Anonymous (Transposed 2nd Tone)*

The cantus contains the second psalm tone (transposed) and the tenor forms sixths below it in the same manner as in *Example 15*. In addition, a mechanical contratenor bassus has been written in alternating fifths and thirds beneath the tenor. Not all of the three-voice settings in *ModC* are so strict in their intervallic successions; this is especially true of the first few Tenebrae psalms (Nos. 49-51). The combinations then become more mechanical in the course of the psalms of *ModC*.

The completion of the change to falsobordone style is reached when a contratenor altus has been added to this basic three-voice structure, whereby the typical falsobordone contains four voices.[1] *Example 17*, is taken from the early sixteenth century manuscript, Barcelona, Biblioteca central, *MS 454*, and illustrates the end result, early falsobordone.

[1] Although falsobordone came to be written in more than four voices later in the sixteenth century, the four-voice style dominates in the early part of the century, and may be regarded as typical for that period.

Example 17. *Barcelona, Bibl. cent.* 454 (*f.* 177*v*) *Dixit, Dominus* 2*us* *Tonus*

As in *Examples 15* and *16*, the second psalm tone is utilised in the cantus, the tenor is added in sixths beneath the cantus, and a mechanical bassus has been added beneath the tenor in alternating thirds and fifths, for the most part.[1] The fourth voice, a contratenor altus, has been added above the tenor in fourths and thirds *not*, it must be emphasised, beneath the cantus in parallel fourths, as had been true of the parallel contratenor altus in early three-voice fauxbourdon; this altus amplifies the harmony. In *Example 17*, the fourths and thirds do not quite alternate strictly, and there is some crossing of the voices. As the altus in Oriola's setting of *In exitu* (*Example 14*), this part seems somewhat more removed from the improvisatory model than the bassus. The completely mechanical succession of intervals that apparently formed the basis for improvisation *supra librum* is illustrated by Guilielmus Monachus in the following *Example 18*.

[1] The octaves formed on the weak beats in measures 3, 7 and 8 punctuating the alternating thirds and fifths represent a common occurrence in Spanish (fabordón) sources. We shall have cause to offer a technical explanation of these octaves in the chapter in Volume II which deals with the fauxbourdon contratenores. The tenth, is of course, the musical equivalent of the third; a composition in which the thirds are not compounded, such as in *Examples 14* and *16*, would seem closer to the improvisatory model.

Example 18. *Strict intervallic structure of four-voice faulx bordon according to Guilielmus Monachus* [1]

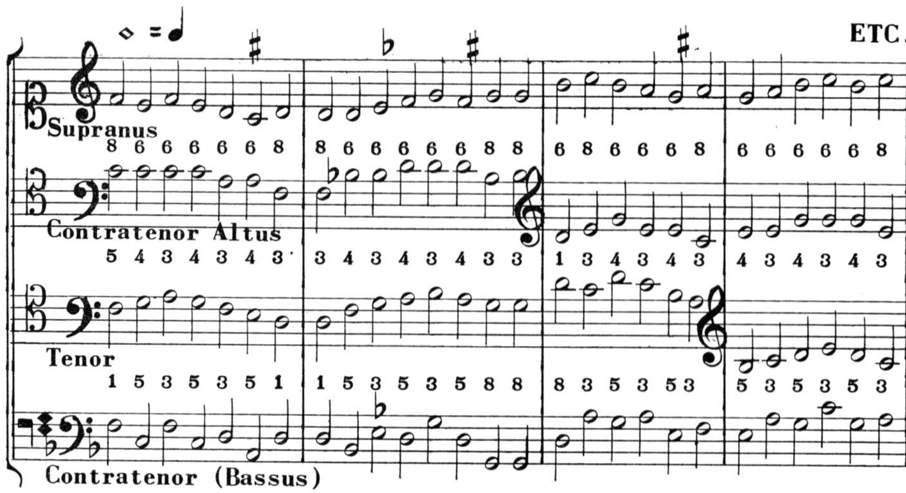

[1] (fol. $31^{r\text{-}v}$) Coussemaker, *Scriptores...*, III, p. 296. The complete title of this treatise is *De preceptis artis musice et practice compendiosus libellus Guilielmi monaci cantoris integerrimi ac viri eruditissimi* and is preserved in the Biblioteca Marciana in Venice, *MS lat. fondo antico N° 336*, *Collocazione 1581*, provenience: Contarini, Giacomo. Part of the original has been published by Coussemaker, *opere citato*, III, pp. 273-307. An errata-list to this edition is included in M. Bukofzer, *Geschichte des englischen Diskants und des Fauxbourdons nach den theoretischen Quellen*, 1936, pp. 153-156. The following is a list of addenda thereto.

Page	Correction
289a	The first two examples should not have been notated on 12 and 10 line staves. Actually, the entire page of the original had been lined in advance of the copying, some lines being used for text, others for music. Only two, normal five-line staves seem to have been intended for the music. This is consistent with the practice observed in the remainder of the treatise. The upper stave has a *C* clef on the fourth line and the lower one a *C* clef on the first line.
	Line of Music (abbreviated as LM henceforth) 1: a semibrevis rest follows the tenor.
	LM 2: a semibrevis rest follows the last note in the soprano.
	LM 2 & 3: no *sight* for the soprano on the last note, or for the altus at the beginning of the next example.
	LT (Line of Text) 3 from bottom: *sextas* instead of *sextam*.
289b	LT 2 from bottom: *et* instead of *ita*.
	LT 1 from bottom: add *exemplum patet vertendo folium*.
290a	In title: add *modum* between *secundum* and *Francigenorum*.
292a	Final LT: add *cum* before *tribus vocibus*.
293a	LT 3: *altus* instead of *alius*.
	LM 7: the eighth note from the end is white.
293b	Fourth paragraph: *Secunda regula*: *Et nota quod si gymel*, etc.
	LT 6 from bottom: *supra tenorem* (as two distinct words).
	LT 2 from bottom: *faulxbordon* instead of *fauxlbordon*.
294a	LM 1: normal semibrevis rests in the original.
	LM 2: final five notes in the tenor: *b flat*, *a*, *g*, *f*, *g*, an octave higher in the original.

It is not specified in the text which voice contains the cantus firmus; evidently, Guilielmus Monachus did not think that it mattered. His voice-pairs, cantus-tenor (8 6 6 6...8), altus-tenor (5 4 3 4 3 4...4 3) and basuss-tenor (5 3 5 3 5...5 8) do not deviate from the established pattern. If the example were to be followed as a model for improvisation *supra librum*, the succession of intervals of the improvised voices would have to be observed closely lest the entire ensemble become mired in dissonance, but when used for written compositions, the formulae did not, obviously, have to be followed so strictly. In this *freer* form, one often finds these successions serving as the basis for composition in falsobordone style. This has been illustrated above in *Examples 14* and *17*.

The occasion of Guilielmus Monachus's theoretical example of intervallic succession formulae moves us to make a systematic examination of all of the possibilities of combining intervals, in order that we may better understand the methods of the fifteenth century in writing *harmonisations* note against note. The formulae actually reflect a very astute perception of the possibilities and opportunities of superimposing intervals on the cantus and tenor of fauxbourdon (or of any duet in sixths and octaves). It is furthermore interesting to examine these methods of the successive composition of voices, so foreign to our contemporary concept of choral composition.

In the first place, in considering the possibilities of adding a bassus to a cantus and tenor in sixths and octaves, one finds that the best intervals to use below a sixth consist of unison, third, fifth and octave (and their octave transpositions),

LM 3: final note *g* instead of *e*.

294b LM 7: add semibreves *a* and *g* at the end of the line, (Bukofzer indicates minimae, but the two notes have been partially corrupted by a foreign hand from semibreves to minimae. They must be semibreves to fit the other part.).

295a LM 1: 14th note should be *a* instead of *g*.

Final LM: the tenth note is actually *g* in the MS, as Coussemaker has indicated it, not *e* as Bukofzer suggests.

296a LT 4 from top and 5 from bottom: *antepenultimam* instead of *antepenultima*.

LT 3 & 4 from bottom: *ita quod ultima sit semper tertia* has been copied only once in the original.

LT 1 & 2 from bottom: *vel octava bassa et prima notula pariter, ut patet per exemplum* was inserted by a later hand, possibly by the same one that renumbered the folios after the treatise was bound in its present form. Since this insertion provides that *non sequitur*, it should be deleted.

296b LT 2: add *est* after *talis*.

LT 3: delete one *mi*.

297a LM 4: The *C* clef on the third line is used in the manuscript, but should be placed on the second line, making the third note a *b-flat* as indicated by Bukofzer. A sharp immediately follows this note.

LM 5: the second group of tenor notes has the succession: *e, e, d, e,* instead of *e, d, e, e*.

297b The cantus of the musical example has a *C* clef on the first line throughout.

298a LM 2: the initial rest has the value of a semibrevis.

LT 4: add *non* between *est* and *diminutum*.

298b LM 5: the 14th and 15th notes are *b-flat* and *c* instead of *a* and *b-flat*; the 17th note is *c* instead of *b-flat*.

306b LT 1: in paragraph concerned with *sincopation*: *semiucem* instead of *semiuncem*.

Mensuration for the example of syncopation is ɔ.

as shown in *Example 19a*, whereas beneath an octave, the best intervals consist of an unison, third, fifth, sixth or octave, as shown in *Example 19b*.

Example 19a.

Example 19b.

In devising a fixed pattern of succession to be memorised and used, the composers of falsobordone tended to delimit this group even more. Only the third and fifth were utilised, possibly, because this would tend best to create harmonic fullness, or because either interval would form a consonance with the octave as well as with the sixth. Perhaps, these thirds and fifths were alternated to avoid parallel fifths and octaves. In any event, a great many falsobordone compositions observe this formula to a greater or lesser extent. The compositions most likely to preserve the fixed intervallic successions with the least amount of variation are those falsobordone formulae for the succession of psalm tones which are preserved in many early sixteenth century manuscripts, especially those of Spanish provenience.

If a composer were actually composing a psalm setting in falsobordone, he could use this mechanical procedure as a point of departure. In the course of the sixteenth century, as we shall discuss, falsobordone gravitated farther and farther from its stereotyped model to become the harmonic style so well-known today, where the reciting tone consists of a single chord followed by a florid cadence.

Examples 19c and *19d* illustrate the method of creating compatibility between a mechanical contratenor bassus and the parallel contratenor altus. A third is possible beneath the tenor which forms a *sixth chord*, but the fifth below would form a dissonance with the fourth below the cantus. Neither fifth nor third is appropriate beneath the open harmony. The fact that the fifth is inappropriate beneath *either* of the only two consonant harmonies of three-voice parallel fauxbourdon renders the parallel altus incompatible with the contratenor bassus. Thus, if a bassus and an altus were to be used in connection with a fauxbourdon cantus and tenor, a new formula would have to be devised to replace that of the older parallel altus.

If a tone, a third rather than a fourth below the cantus, is inserted between the cantus and tenor in sixths, it makes possible the addition of the necessary fifth below in the bass as well as the third, as shown here in *Example 19e*.

Example 19c.

Example 19d.

Example 19e.

The fifth below is especially needed for the penultimate chord of the cadence, as Guilielmus Monachus had specifically noted [1] and as is illustrated in *Example 18*. Thus, in order to fit into the pattern of the contratenor bassus, the altus must form thirds below the cantus (= fourths above the tenor) in addition to the fourths below the cantus that had been a feature of the parallel altus. This altus, alternating intervals as it did, presented a problem of synchronisation, because the third above the tenor must be coïncidental with the third below, and the fourth above must sound with the fifth below if the formulae are to be concordant. The formula for the bassus did not involve this synchronisation except at cadences where the fifth below the tenor was necessary to the penultimate harmony. The amplifying altus, however, increased the chances for error when singing *supra librum*. Somewhat later, in the second half of the sixteenth century, the anonymous Scotch author in British Museum, *Additional MS 4911*, presented a simplification of the altus by eliminating the thirds above the tenor, leaving only the parallel fourths above the tenor.[2] We shall discuss this method at greater length later; suffice it to say at this point that the notated examples adduced by this Scotch author apply fourths above the tenor for the most part, but there are some notable exceptions; we find some fifths and the final interval forms a (major) third. Adrian Petit Coclico also illustrates this method in his *Exemplum aliud quatuor vocum Faulbourdon* (= what we have termed falsobordone), but does not describe it in his text.[3]

Although these formulae have been known for quite some time, their importance to the history of fauxbourdon-falsobordone has not been sufficiently investigated. Actually, they show us the only direct connection in the development of the later style from the earlier one. We see, from evidence found in Oriola's setting of *In exitu* (*Example 14*) and from the formula for the second psalm tone illustrated in *Example 17*, that falsobordone style was achieved through

[1] *Confer* pp. 46-47.

[2] (fol. 104^{v}) The ferd kynd of Faburdoun is of four partis quhair the baritonant (*id est*, bassus) is set in thirds, fyfts, octavis beneth the planesang, or in unison with the plane sang. And the plane sang is modulat in the propir seit. As be thir exemplis followand the way and proces of this put kynd of Faburdoun may perfytly be understand.

[3] *Compendium musices*, (Nuremberg, 1552), fol. 52^{v}.

the addition of a bassus and an amplifying altus to a cantus and tenor in sixths.

The usual technical explanation of the genesis of falsobordone quite often presents the relationship of falsobordone to fauxbourdon as being evinced by the *sixth chords* which *frequently* occur in the three voices of fauxbourdon.[1] This hypothosis holds that the metamorphosis was completed when a fourth voice, a *free* bassus, was added to the cantus, parallel altus and tenor of fauxbourdon. The aptness of this explanation hinges on the word *frequently*. Its principal fallacy has been unconsciously demonstrated in the *Harvard Dictionary of Music*,[2] the only major reference work to attempt to present a musical example to document this theory. The illustration, the source of which is omitted, has been taken from Cabezón's, *Obras de música para tecla arpa y vihuela*,[3] and is an example of keyboard, not vocal, falsobordone. Seven of the fourteen consonant harmonies formed by the upper three voices in the Cabezón composition are in second, not first inversion. There are only *three* chords in first inversion! One would rather say, on the basis of this composition, that the six-three chords are rather infrequently formed in the upper three voices of falsobordone. One can readily see that the upper three voices of our *Examples 14* and *17*, as well as of the composition by Cabezón, do not form merely one type of chord, but contain rather a mixture. Probably, there are more of the type of chords which we should term second inversion than any other, but these do not overwhelm the others. This is the rule in falsobordone, as it is in most other types of compositions which move note against note.

Exploring this question further, we find that *ModC* provides us, rather unexpectedly, with documentary evidence to solidify our thesis. An exceptional four-voice setting of the Magnificat by Iohannes Martini (*ModC* 46) does actually utilise sixth chords in the upper voices throughout. The cantus and tenor are provided with a *faulx bordon* inscription as in an ordinary fauxbourdon composition, but this composition is unusual because it adds a notated contratenor bassus, as illustrated in *Example 20*.

[1] Guido Adler, *Studie zur Geschichte der Harmonie*, in the *Sitzungsberichte der philosophisch-historischen Klasse der kaiserlichen Akademie der Wissenschaften in Wien*, Volume XCVIII, Heft III, 1881, p. 826.

[2] Willi Apel, *Harvard Dictionary of Music*, 1947, p. 261a, Example 5.

[3] Transcribed in *Hispaniae scholae musica sacra*, Volumes III, IV, VII and VIII, edidit F. Pedrell. The fabordones are contained in Volume III, pp. 32-47.

Example 20. *ModC* 46 *Magnificat* (8*th tone*), 10. *Martini*

The bassus in this example has been added beneath the tenor according to the formula: 3 8 3 8 3 8 etc., which is somewhat of a variant from the formula 3 5 3 5 3 5 8 suggested by Guilielmus Monachus. Nevertheless, it is strictly carried out and is definitely related to the normal case. Actually, it is an ingenious solution for a difficult technical problem (*confer Examples 19c* and *d*, *supra* p. 59). Whereas one can find many falsobordoni with a mixture of different types of chords in the upper three voices together with alternating thirds and fifths between the bassus and tenor,[1] the formula used here by Martini does not seem to have been applied in the later style. One reason for this may involve the rather difficult technical problems encountered. We shall have cause again later to examine another, much earlier composition of this type contained in the second section, the French part, of *Tr 87*; this is a setting of the *Gloria* by an anonymous composer who lacked much of Martini's skill. The resulting, rather awkward setting is interesting chiefly because it emphasises the difficulties in writing convincingly in this doubly circumscribed style.

In Martini's setting of the Magnificat, we find one of the difficulties at cadential points. The fourth below the cantus produces the surprising sound, which we should describe as a dominant seventh, in the penultimate chord of the cadence. For several reasons, therefore, the compositional technique applied by Martini in this Magnificat must be regarded as experimental and without important influence for the further course of development of falsobordone.

In surveying the results of our study of the fauxbourdon settings and duets in sixths in *ModC*, we see that, in contradistinction to *ModB*, the compositions in *ModC* have 1) begun to turn away from hymns (*id est* melodic compositions) in favour of psalms (based on recitation formulae), 2) simplified the melodic style of both voices, 3) added a text to the tenor, and 4) decreased the rhythmic independence of the voices by increasing the adoption of the note-against-note style. The final characteristics still to be achieved in consumating the change to falsobordone involve the addition of an amplifying altus and the writing out of all the voices.

Table 6 below compares the characteristics of the fauxbourdon in *ModC* with those in the earlier sources. Only three of the original characteristics remain: 1) the sixth and the octave continue as the basic consonances, 2) the melodic succession is still determined by the cantus firmus located in the uppermost voice, and 3) the term *faulx bordon* is still used as a vernacular *canon*.

One important element stands out; the use of unnotated alternate contratenores observing restricted and patterned intervallic successions has been vastly extended in the later source. The fact that this practice sprang from a canonic device whereby it was used primarily in music of a quasi-improvisational nature accounts

[1] In addition to *Examples 14* and *17*, numerous other transcriptions of falsobordone are available in print, *exempli gratia* Pedrell edidit, *Hispaniae scholae musica sacra*, Volume VI, pp. 15, 20-22 and 56-59; H. Anglés, *La Música en la corte de los reyes católicos*, III, *Polifonia profana* No. 418 (Monumento X) (Old edition by F. A. Barbieri, *Cancionero musical de los siglos XV y XVI*, No. 307, 1890). Falsobordoni by Italian composers are transcribed in *Musica Divina*, Volume IV, pp. 261-262, edidit Carl Proske, 1863.

TABLE 6. COMPARISON OF EARLY AND LATE FAUXBOURDON

	Early	Late
1.	Triple meter.	Duple meter.
2.	Counter rhythms.	Note against note.
3.	Partially melismatic.	Syllabic.
4.	Text in cantus only.	Text in all voices.
5.	Hymns most popular.	Psalms most popular.
6.	Melodic chants used for cantus firmi.	Reciting tones used for cantus firmi.
7.	All non-harmonic tones used.	Only suspension and/or anticipation used in cadences.
8.	"Landini" cadence.	Suspension cadence.
9.	3 or 4 consecutive sixths usual.	Parallel sixths throughout phrases.
10.	One contratenor.	Three different contratenores ad libitum.
11.	Three voices.	Three or four voices.

for the fact that the contratenores, in these cases, were not notated. The technique of fauxbordon exerted a powerful influence on many other types of improvisational music of the late fifteenth and early sixteenth centuries, sacred and secular, instrumental and vocal. The fact that the contratenores were not notated also accounts for the relative paucity of knowledge about them.[1] One finds evidence of the practice of fauxbourdon and falsobordone in more popular types of music such as in frottole and villancicos. We shall have cause to discuss the use of the formulae in secular forms and styles later; at present, we are interested primarily in the intervallic succession of the voices of fauxbourdon and falsobordone.

The practice is entirely consistent with the canonic ancestry of fauxbourdon, and was undoubtedly the inevitable result of the combination of Franco-Flemish ingenuity and the technique of successive composition of voices, that eventually produced a system of combining voices in repetitive patterns in a manner somewhat analogous to the repetition of tonal successions and durational values in the isorhythmic motet. The result, as has been pointed out before, is a contrapuntal device similar in technique to invertible counterpoint. The detailed study of these voices that were so intimately connected with the practice of composing voices

[1] They are not mentioned by Ernst Ferand either in *Die Improvisation in der Musik*, 1938, or in the article *Improvisation* in the encyclopedia *Die Musik in Geschichte und Gegenwart*, nor are they discussed by Emil Haraszti in his recent article *La Technique des improvisateurs de langue vulgaire et de latin au quattrocento*, in the *Revue belge de musicologie*, VIII 1954, pp. 12-31. Both Laurence Feininger in *Die Frühgeschichte des Kanons* (Dissertation, Heidelberg, 1937) and Walter Blankenburg in the article *Kanon* in *Die Musik in Geschichte und Gegenwart* mention the use of the *canon* in fauxbourdon but go into no further detail. The writers of more specialised studies of fauxbourdon have concentrated their attention more on the parallel altus because of its formation of chords of the sixth and have ignored the other formulae.

seriatim is an indispensible aid in revealing the implications of this compositional method so foreign to the harmonic way of thinking of the eighteenth and nineteenth centuries.[1]

To create a fauxbourdon, one must begin with a cantus firmus. In the actual fauxbourdon that have come down to us, the cantus firmus is almost invariably in the uppermost voice. In a fauxbourdon *supra librum*, however, the cantus firmus could apparently be left unornamented and sung at the indicated tonal level in the tenor part, or could be transposed and put into the soprano.[2] One would add a tenor in lower sixths to the cantus, or, if the cantus firmus was in the tenor, upper sixths to form a cantus. Octaves would be used, in either case, at the beginnings of phrases and for final consonances. The result is illustrated to some extent in *Example 21a*. To this framework of parallel sixths, we should add the different contratenores seriatim. When a parallel altus is added, as in *Example 21b*, one obtains a series of *chords* (or harmonies) in first inversion. Harmonically, the succession is not functional because of the similarity of the root progression to the melodic movement of the voices.

Example 21a.

Example 21b.

The effect of this could be said to be fuller but not more functional as harmony. This type of setting is, of course, well known today, but it did not monopolise

[1] Some branches of contemporary music which use all twelve tones of the chromatic scale may herald a return to the successive method of composition. Students of the late Arnold Schönberg, for example, have reported that Schönberg analysed each line of their compositions seriatim, committing it to memory and thereby gradually building up a tonal impression of the entire composition. This method is indicative of Schönberg's preoccupation with linear movement.

[2] Our interpretation of the illustration of *faulxbordon* in Guilielmus Monachus's treatise (Coussemaker, *Scriptores*..., III, p. 288, facsimile in *Die Musik in Geschichte und Gegenwart*, V, Plate 49 facing columns 1057-1058) differs from others found in the scientific literature. Bukofzer, for example, claimed quite categorically that this was a specimen of *English discant*, because the cantus firmus was contained in the tenor, and that Guilielmus Monachus had erroneously termed this *faulxbordon* (*Geschichte*..., especially pp. 58-65 and *Musical Quarterly*, XXXVIII 1952, p. 45 footnote 35). J. Handschin maintained that it did not make any difference in which voice the cantus firmus was placed, the difference in the total effect was quite negligible when the cantus firmus was moved from voice to voice (*Eine umstrittene Stelle bei Guilielmus Monachus*, in the *Bericht über den Kongress der Internationalen Gesellschaft für Musikwissenschaft in Basel, 1949*, 1950, p. 148. We shall develop our reasons in support of Handschin's thesis in Volume II in the chapters devoted to Improvisation and the opinions of the theorists regarding fauxbourdon.

Guilielmus Monachus's attention. He also describes a setting for three voices with a cantus, tenor and bassus without altus, as illustrated in *Example 21c*, as well as a setting for four voices with a cantus, tenor and bassus as well as an (amplifying) altus, as shown in *Example 21d.*

Example 21 c. **Example 21 d.**

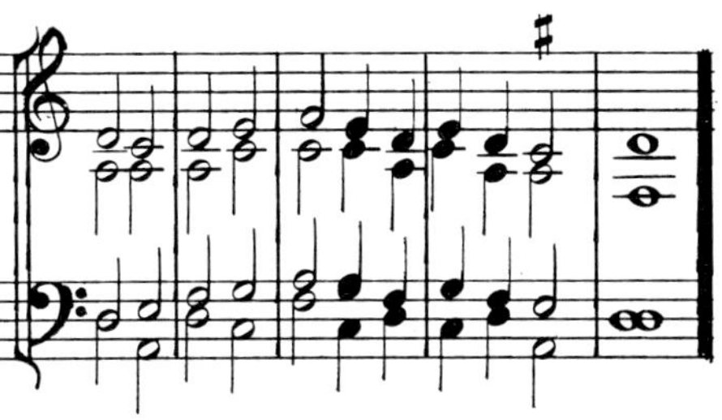

Thus, one can obtain three different styles of fauxbourdon simply by changing the contratenor. If one omits the contratenor entirely, one obtains a fourth style, which Guilielmus Monachus would have termed *gymel*, as illustrated in *Example 21a.* The *gymel* is, thus, the unchanging framework of fauxbourdon to which the contratenores are added, *si placent.*

Unlike the setting with a parallel contratenor altus, the fauxbourdon style with the contratenor bassus exhibits a great deal of functional harmonic logic particularly at cadences with its semblances of a dominant tonic relationship. This progression, it must be remembered, was achieved through rules of melodic succession not, as in the present day, by chord structure and root progression. The very fact that Guilielmus Monachus used a melodic approach to an harmonic goal was symptomatic of the gradual change enveloping music; in earlier, polyphonic music, the successive composition of voices had reigned supreme, whereas in the sixteenth century, the implied chordal concepts inherent in the music of the time became formalised even in theoretical treatises, as, for example, in the *De Istitutione harmoniche* of Gioseffo Zarlino (Venice, 1558).

Guilielmus Monachus had felt it important enough to insist upon a quasi dominant-tonic relationship at crucial points such as phrase endings, for he specified that the fifth below the tenor should always from the penultimate interval, moving then to the octave or unison of the final. G. Adler [1] utilised this facet of falsobordone coupled with the fact that the bassus alternates thirds and

[1] *Opere citato*, p. 826: *Wenn also der Bass als harmonische Füllstimme in regelrechter Weise seine Entwicklung nahm, so galt der Gesang doch noch immer als Falso Bordone und dies auch noch, als ein regelmässiger vierstimmiger Gesang sich aus dem dreistimmigen gebildet hatte.* On the preceding page, Adler had estimated the time elapsed between the style of parallel fauxbourdon and four voice fauxbourdon (*id est*, falsobordone) as 200 years. Since Adler believed that Guilielmus Monachus's treatise had been formulated circa 1400, it must needs follow that Adler felt that fauxbourdon was initially developed around 1200. This erroneous opinion still enjoys some favour today.

fifths below the tenor as the overall decisive factors in estimating the importance of the bassus and the amplifying altus in the writings of Guilielmus Monachus. Although its systematic intervallic characteristics have not previously been discussed extensively, the existence of an harmonic, falsobordone bassus has been an accepted historical fact for some time. The question must still be answered as to when it first appeared.

In surveying the extant music of fauxbourdon, we are surprised by a systematic, *falsobordone* bassus in the relatively early source, Florence, Biblioteca nazionale centrale, *manuscritti Magliabecchiani XIX, 112bis* (*FM*) dating from around the middle of the fifteenth century and slightly later than *ModB*, the first important manuscript to record the stylistic change to parallel fauxbourdon. In *FM*, a setting by Antonius Janue of the processional hymn, *Gloria laus*,[1] significantly, presents the same simplified style of fauxbourdon that one had found in the parallel antiphons in *ModB* with duple meter and vocal tenores (*confer supra* pp. 36ff.). It appears, thus, that the stylistic simplification and the systematic fauxbourdon bassus were developed at approximately the same time, and we might infer that there is a direct relationship between these two phenomena; we shall have cause to return to this question later.[2]

The new bassus was an alternate *resolutio* of the intervallic succession *canon*. Alternate contratenores themselves had formed integral parts of the fauxbourdon style almost from its inception, as evidenced by the contratenores *sine* fauxbourdon discussed previously. Since the tenor was provided with text in the newer style, the bassus apparently is derived from that voice. The addition of an unnotated, canonic part with *alternating* rather than continuous intervals is reflected in the simplification of the melodic and rhythmic ornamentation of the voices. The new fauxbourdon contratenor is, thus, the result of the combining of two different ideas: 1) intervallic succession peculiar to fauxbourdon, as defined in its *canon*, and 2) low pitched contratenores, as used in other musical compositions. The early fifteenth century compositions with low contratenores, which Besseler [3] investigated, provide impressive evidence for the apparent interest in developing a bass part shown by several composers including Dufay. Actually, Dufay's compositions prove to be the most interesting in this regard, because his concept of the low voice was the most imaginative and the voice itself the most functional. The mechanical fauxbourdon contratenor bassus was simply a canonic manifestation of this bass. It is not unreasonable that a new solution for the *faulx bourdon canon* should have been devised, since the device itself had become popular and had created a great following of interest, which led inevitably to further

[1] Only the stanza *Israël, tu es rex* has the notated contratenor bassus, but both the refrain, *Gloria laus*, and the strophe have an inscription *A faulx bordon*. Thus, the composer (or scribe) took great care to note that the bassus was also *A faulx bordon*.

[2] The manuscript *CS 15*, which contains a répertoire from the late fifteenth and early sixteenth centuries, contains, for example, one of the antiphons from *ModB*, Dufay's *Petrus Apostolus*, with the mechanically derived bassus notated in full (together with the amplifying altus).

[3] Besseler, *Bourdon und Fauxbourdon*, Chapter III, especially the tables on pp. 28, 47 and 53.

experimentation with the possibilities inherent in an intervallic succession *canon*. Creativity, thus, was even able to be applied to such an inflexible device as fauxbourdon.

Having established our historical thesis on the basis of the primary sources, we shall continue in *Volume II* by analysing and discussing the fauxbourdon compositions in the secondary and peripheral sources.

APPENDIX I - ANALYTICAL INDEX

The compositions in the *Analytical Index* are grouped according to liturgical function and are listed in alphabetical order, settings of the Kyrie being arranged by their tropes and Magnificats by their tones.

Symbols in the column *Meter and Voices* refer constantly to notated parts; *P* indicates that only part of the polyphonic setting specifies fauxbourdon; the mensuration and number of voices given apply only to such sections. It should be noted that fully half of the compositions include sections for two or three *free* polyphonic voices in addition to fauxbourdon. No attempt has been made to indicate any alternation between fauxbourdon and plainchant, which is included in the more complete sources, such as *BL* and *CS 15*; quite often the odd-numbered verses are to be sung monophonically.

Basic fauxbourdon with a cantus and tenor and inscription is indicated by a *2* in the column *Meter and Voices*. Auxiliary voices are indicated in the following manner:

- 3s Cantus, tenor and contratenor *sine faulx bourdon*.
- 3B Cantus, tenor and contratenor bassus.
- 3A Cantus, tenor and contratenor altus.
- 4T Cantus, fauxbourdon tenor, non-fauxbourdon tenor and non-fauxbourdon contratenor.
- 4Ct Cantus, tenor, contratenor altus and contratenor bassus.

Auxiliary voices found in only some of the manuscripts are described in the footnotes. An asterisk * preceding an entry indicates that the fauxbourdon inscription is wanting.

References are made to the following publications, *inc* indicating that only a partial transcription is offered.

1. BesselerBF — Heinrich Besseler, *Bourdon und Fauxbourdon*, 1950.
2. BesselerUF — Heinrich Besseler, *Der Ursprung des Fauxbourdons*, in *Die Musikforschung*, I 1948, pp. 106-112.
3. BukofzerF — Manfred Bukofzer, *Fauxbourdon Revisited*, in the *Musical Quarterly*, XXXVIII 1952, pp. 22-47.
4. BukofzerP — Manfred Bukofzer, *Popular Polyphony in the Middle Ages*, in the *Musical Quarterly*, XXVI 1940, pp. 31 ff.
5. BukofzerS — Manfred Bukofzer, *Studies in Medieval and Renaissance Music*, 1950.
6. DCS — *Desoff Choir Series*, edidit Paul Boepple.

7. DTÖ VII — *Sechs Trienter Codices*, erste Auswahl, in the *Denkmäler der Tonkunst in Oesterreich*, Jahrgang VII, 1900, edideunt ADLER and KOLLER.
8. DTÖ Bd. 53 — *Sechs Trienter Codices*, vierte Auswahl, in the *Denkmäler der Tonkunst in Oesterreich*, Band LIII, 1920, edideunt R. VON FICKER and A. OREL.
9. DTÖ Bd. 61 — *Sechs Trienter Codices*, fünfte Auswahl, in the *Denkmäler der Tonkunst in Oesterreich*, Band LXI, 1924, edidit R. VON FICKER.
10. DufayO — G. DUFAY, *Opera omnia*, edidit G. de VAN, Vol. I-IV, 1947 *et sequens*; this series will be continued under the editorship of HEINRICH BESSELER.
11. GerberDH — *G. Dufay, sämtliche Hymnen*, edidit RUDOLF GERBER, in *Das Chorwerk*, IL.
12. GerberIH — RUDOLF GERBER, *Zur italienischen Hymnenkompositionen im 15. Jahrhundert*, in the *Acta musicologica*, XXVIII, 1956, pp. 78-82.
13. GerberRH — RUDOLF GERBER, *Römische Hymnenzyklen des späten 15 Jahrhunderts*, in the *Archiv für Musikwissenschaft*, XII 1955, pp. 40-73.
14. Harrison — FRANK LL. HARRISON, *Music in Medieval Britain*, 1958.
15. Marix — JEANNE MARIX, *Les Musiciens de la cour de Bourgogne au XVe siècle*, 1937.
16. Miller — CATHERINE K. MILLER, *The Early English Carol*, in *Renaissance News*, III 1950, pp. 61-64.
17. Wolf — JOHANNES WOLF, *Music of Earlier Times*, sine die.
18. WolfGdM — JOHANNES WOLF, *Geschichte der Mensuralnotation*, I-III, 1904.

A list of the manuscript sigla is found on page 6. The division of certain manuscripts is made in the following fashion:

1. *Em*(B) = the section of *Em* in black notation; numbers 17-156.
   Em(W) = the section of *Em* in white notation; numbers 1-16 & 157-276.
2. *Tr 87*(I) = the first section of *Trent Codex 87*, numbers 1-162.
   Tr 87(II) = the second section of *Trent Codex 87*, numbers 163-198.
3. *Tr 92*(I) = Trent Codex *92*, first section; numbers 1365-1509.
   Tr 92(II) = Trent Codex *92*, second section; numbers 1510-1589.
4. *BL* (N) indicates those compositions which were added by the second hand of the manuscript (*confer* the facsimile in *Musica Disciplina*, II 1948, facing page 233. The handwriting of the first scribe is illustrated in the facsimile facing page 232).

	Title - Composer	Meter & Voices	Published
1.	Ad coenam, Dufay	(O) p2 [4]	GerberDH 7b
2.	Ad coenam, Lymburgia	(O) p2	BukofzerF 43 inc
3.	Aures ad, Anonymous	₵ p4ct.	GerberRH 63 inc
4.	Ave maris, Anonymous	₵ 2	
5.	Ave maris, Dufay	(O) 3s	GerberDH 15 [7]
6.	Christe redemptor[1], Dufay	(O) 2	
7.	Christe redemptor[1], Dufay	(O) 2	GerberDH 2, DTÖ VII 160
8.	Conditor alme, Dufay	(O) 2	GerberDH 1, DTÖ VII 161
9.	Cultor dei, Anonymous	(O) p1	
10.	Deus tuorum [2], Dufay	(O) 2	GerberDH 19
11.	Exultet celum, Dufay	(O) 4T	GerberDH 18a
12.	Festum nunc, Anonymous	(O) 2	
13.	Gloria laus, Anonymous	(O) 2	
14.	Gloria laus, Janue	₵ 2 & 3B	GerberIH 81-82 inc
15.	Hostis Herodes, Anonymous	(O) 4T	
16.	Iste confessor, Anonymous	₵ 2	
17.	Iste confessor, Anonymous	₵ p4Ct.	
18.	Iste confessor, Dufay	(O) 2	GerberDH 21
19.	Iste confessor, Janue	₵ 2	GerberIH 80 inc
20.	Jesu corona, Anonymous	Ø 2	
21.	Jesu corona [3], Dufay	(O) 2	(GerberDH) 19
22.	Jesu corona, Janue	(O) 2	GerberIH 80 inc
23.	Jesu nostra red., Anonymous	₵ 2	
24.	Lucis creator, Anonymous	O p4Ct.	
25.	Lucis creator, Benoit	(O) 3s	BukofzerPP 47
26.	Lucis creator, Feraguti	O 2	
27.	Magne dies, Lymburgia	(O) 3s	
28.	Pange lingua, Merques	O 2	DTÖ Bd. 53 84
29.	Pange lingua, Anonymous	O 4T	
30.	Rex gloriose, Roullet	(O) 2	
31.	Salve festa dies, Anonymous	(O) 2	
32.	Salva festa dies, Anonymous	(O) 2	
33.	Te Deum, Binchois	(O) 2	Marix 14
34.	Tibi Christe, Benoyt	O 2	
35.	Tibi Christe, Dufay	(O) 2	
36.	Urbs beata, Anonymous	O p2	
37.	Ut queant, Anonymous	(O) 2	
38.	Ut queant, Binchois	O 2 [5]	Wolf (after *Ven*)
39.	Ut queant, Janue	(O) 2	GerberIH 78 inc
40.	Ut queant, Ray. de Lan	(O) 2	

	Title - Composer	Meter & Voices	Published
41.	Veni creator, Dufay	O p4T	
42.	Veni creator, Binchois	(O) 2	DTÖ Bd. 53 89
43.	Verbum supernum, Anonymous	(Ȼ) 2	
44.	Vexilla regis, Anonymous	Ȼ p4Ct.	
45.	Vexilla regis, Dufay	O p4T [6]	GerberDH 6b
46.	Virginis proles, Lymburgia	(O) 2	

[1] The music of Dufay's *Christe redemptor... ex patre*, *BL* (N) 295 is the same as for *Christe redemptor conserva*, *BL* (N) 305.

[2] The music of Dufay's *Deus tuorum* is the same as that for his *Jesu corona*, *id est* *BL* (N) 311 = *BL* (N) 315 and *ModB* 23 = *ModB* 25.

[3] The music of Dufay's *Jesu corona* is the same as that for his *Deus tuorum*, *id est* *BL* (N) 315 = *BL* (N) 311 and *ModB* 25 = *ModB* 23.

[4] Odd-numbered verses are for three *free voices*, even-numbered verses are set in fauxbourdon. *Tr 89* 745 and *CS 15* 9 (fol. 23v-24r) contain three-voice versions; *confer* GerberDH 7a for the more extended form. *ModB* 9 presents both versions.

[5] (Cantus) and tenor are written out in *Em*; (contratenor altus) and tenor are written out in *Ven*; together the three different voices form a complete fauxbourdon with a contratenor altus.

[6] A non-fauxbourdon version for three *free* voices is found in *ModB* 8, *Ca* 29 (f. 258v), *MC* p. 299 and *Tr 92* (I) 1428 (*confer* GerberDH 6a). The fauxbourdon tenor, found only in *CS 15*, was probably not written by Dufay.

[7] GerberDH Appendix No. 4 offers a transcription of *Tr 92* (II) 1579, which is composed of Dufay's cantus and a later, anonymous non-fauxbourdon tenor and contratenor for *Ave maris stella*.

Hymn	BL	Em	Trent	FM	ModB	CS 15 [5]	_Miscellaneous & No Inscription_
1.			_89_ 744		9		
2.	(N) 297						
3.						7, St2	
4.							_Ver 759_ 45
5.	(N) 304	(W) 157					*_CS 15_ 15 St2 & _BU_ 21
6.	(N) 305						
7.	(N) 295		_92_(I) 1493		2 [4]	2, St2	_SP_ f. 182 & *_MC_ p. 295
8.	(N) 293	(W) 166 [1]	_92_(I) 1416		1	1, St6	
9.							_Ca_ 29 f. 159
10.	(N) 311				23	*22, St2 [6]	
11.	(N) 310	(B) 136 [2]		13 [2]	21	21, St2	
12.		(W) 4					
13.			_90_ 1066				
14.				36			
15.		(W) 257					
16.							_Ver 759_ 40
17.						26, St2	
18.	(N) 313		_92_(II) 1582		24	*25, St2 [7]	
19.				16			*_MC_ p. 326
20.							_SP_ f. 188
21.	(N) 315				25	*27, St4 [8]	
22.				6a			
23.			_88_ 370				
24.						5, St2	
25.					20		
26.	(N) 301						
27.	(N) 282						
28.			_92_(I) 1415				
29.		(W) 176 [3]					
30.		(W) 163	_87_(I) 11				
31.		(W) 259					
32.			_88_ 365				
33.					*27		SP f. 242^{v} _Mil 2269_ 86 _Ver 761_ f. 222^{v}-225^{r}
34.							_Ven_ 25

Hymn	BL	Em	Trent	FM ModB	CS 15 [5]	*Miscellaneous & No Inscription*
35.	(N) 307					
36.					28, St2	
37.			*92*(1) 1480			
38.		*(W) 171				*Ven* 25
39.				7		
40.						*MüL* 12
41.					11, St2 [9]	
42.			*92*(1) 1385			
43.						*Ca* 29 f. 142v
44.					8, St4	
45.					*8, St2	
46.	(N) 314					

[1] *Amen* set in tenths (precluding a fauxbourdon altus).
[2] *Em* (B) 136 and *FM* 13 present only the cantus and fauxbourdon tenor. *Em* (B) 141 and *SP* f. 187v contain a version for three voices with cantus, tenor and contratenor (*sine fauxbourdon*); these latter versions have been transcribed in GerberDH No. 18b.
[3] This anonymous setting of *Pange lingua* is provided with a fauxbourdon tenor only in *Em*, where it is to be used in connection with the contratenor, which contains the cantus firmus, rather than the cantus.
[4] A *contratenor sine fauxbourdon* has been added in *ModB*.
[5] In *CS 15*, all fauxbourdon compositions are only partially inscribed *A* faulx bordon (sic!).
[6] An anonymous tenor and contratenor (*sine faulx bourdon*) have been added to Dufay's cantus and fauxbourdon tenor, and are transcribed in GerberDH Appendix No. 5b; similarly, No. 5a presents a transcription of *SP* f. 185, which consists of Dufay's cantus with a new, anonymous tenor and contratenor (*sine faulx bourdon*).
[7] *CS 15* 25 presents two additional voices, a non-fauxbourdon contratenor and tenor together with Dufay's original cantus and fauxbourdon tenor. The *canon* must have been utilised at one time in the history of this composition since the four voices are not generally concordant; a different, anonymous tenor and contratenor are transcribed in GerberDH Appendix No. 6; these are still further voices composed anonymously to the cantus of strophe 4 *Unde nunc* of Dufay's *Iste confessor*.
[8] In *CS 15* 27, strophe 4, *Te deprecamur*, presents Dufay's cantus and fauxbourdon tenor without *canon*. Strophe 5, *Laus honor*, uses the same two voices and adds two anonymous contratenores, altus and bassus. A transcription of the four-voice version is contained in GerberDH Appendix No. 7b. GerberDH Appendix No. 7a comprises the second strophe of the same hymn, *Qui pascia*, where an anonymous, non-fauxbourdon tenor and contratenor have been added to Dufay's cantus. GerberDH No. 19 has the text of *Deus tuorum* underlaid, *quod vide*.
[9] The fauxbourdon tenor in *CS 15* was apparently not composed by Dufay. There is a version for three voices *sine fauxbourdon* in *ModB*, *BL*, *FM*, *SP*, *Tr 92*, *Em* & *MC*. A transcription is included in GerberDH No. 9 and Wolf p. 37.

Title and Composer	Meter & Voices	ModC	Ver 759 & Trent 90
47. Benedictus Dominus, Anonymous (Canticle of Zachary)	(C) 2	63	
48. Cantemus Domino, Anonymous (Canticle of Moses)	(C) 2	61	
49. Confitebimur tibi, Anonymous	(C) 2	55	
50. Confitebor, Anonymous	C p2		*Ver 759* 63 (f. 80v-82r)
51. Conserva me, Domine, Anonymous	C 2	77	
52. Cum invocarem, Anonymous	C 2	75	
53. Deus in nomine, Anonymous	(C) 2	69	
54. Deus iudicium, Anonymous	(C) 2	52	
55. Deus ultionum, Anonymous	C p2	72	
56. Dixit Dominus, Anonymous	O p2		*Ver 759* 62 (f. 79v-80r)
57. Domine, audivi, Anonymous (Canticle of Habacus)	C 2	74	
58. Domine, Deus sal., Anonymous	(C) p2	71	
59. Domine est terra, Anonymous	C 2	78	
60. Domine, exaudi, Anonymous	C 2	73	
61. Domine, quis, Anonymous	C 2	76	
62. Domine, refugium, Anonymous	C p2	59	
63. Dominus illuminatio, Anonymous	C p2	66	
64. Domine, ne in furore, Anonymous	(C) p2	67	
65. Eripe me de inimicis, Anonymous	(C) p2	70	
66. Exaltabo te, Domine, Anonymous	C 2	79	
67. Expectans expectavi, Anonymous	(C) 2	68	
68. In exitu Israël, Anonymous	O p2		*Tr 90* 1095
69. In exitu Israël, Anonymous	(O) 2		*Tr 90* 1096
70. Iudica me, Anonymous	C 2	80	
71. Lauda Ierusalem, Anonymous	₵ 2		*Ver 759* 70 (f. 87v-88r)
72. Laudate pueri, Anonymous	O p2		*Ver 759* 65 (f. 83v 84r)
73. Nisi Dominus, Anonymous	₵ 2		*Ver 759* 69 (f. 87v-88r)
74. Notus in Iudea, Anonymous	(C) p2	56	
75. Quam bonus, Anonymous [1]	(C) p2	53	
76. Ut quid per te, Anonymous	C p2	54	
77. Voce mea, Anonymous	C 2	57	

[1] Transcribed in BukofzerS p. 182ff, others unpublished.

MAGNIFICATS (CANTICLES OF THE BLESSED VIRGIN)

Title and Composer	Meter & Voices	Trent	FM	ModB/C	Miscellaneous
78. 1^{i} toni, Anonymous	O & ₵ p2				*Em*(W) 179
79. 1^{i} toni, Anonymous	₵ p2				*SP* f. 191^{v}ff.
80. 1^{i} toni, Anonymous	Ø p2	*88* 243			
81. 1^{i} toni, Anonymous	(O) 2				*Em*(B) 154
82. 1^{i} toni, Anonymous	C 2			*C* 47	
83. 1^{i} toni, Anonymous	₵ p3A	**90* 1042	39		**Tr 92*(I) 1380
84. 1^{i} toni, C. Anthony[1]	₵ p2	*90* 1090			*Tr 93* 1600
85. 2^{i} toni, Feraguti	(O) 2	**90* 1093			*BL*(N) 324
86. 2^{i} toni, Lymburgia	(Ø) 2				*BL*(N) 319
87. 2^{i} toni, Martini	C 3B			*C* 46	*CS 15* 32
88. 4^{i} toni, Anonymous	(O) 2	*87* 87			
89. 6^{i} toni, Anonymous	₵ p2	*90* 1003			
90. 6^{i} toni, Anonymous	(O) 2	*87* 85			
91. 6^{i} toni, Anonymous	(O) 2	*87* 86			
92. 6^{i} toni, Anonymous	₵ p2				*CS 15* 39
93. 6^{i} toni, Arnulphus	C 2				*Vm^{7} 676* 63
94. 7^{i} toni, Anonymous	₵ p2				*CS 15* 40
95. 7^{i} toni, Janue	(O) p2		43		
96. 8^{i} toni, Anonymous	C 2			*C* 44	
97. 8^{i} toni, Dufay	O p2	*92*(I) 1371	22[2]	*B* 36	*SP* f. 211

INTROITS

Title and Composer	Meter & Voices	Em	Trent[3] & Misc.	Ao
98. Benedicta sit, Anonymous	(O) 2		*92*(I) 1395	
99. Cibavit eos, Brasart	(O) p2		*92*(II) 1533	10
100. Da pacem, C. Merques	(O) 2		*92*(I) 1430	12
101. Da ventre, Brasart	(O) p2			
102. Dilexisti, Brasart	(O) p2			16
103. Gaudeamus, Anonymous	C p2	(W) 230		

[1] Transcribed in Harrison p. 347 inc.

[2] The contratenor for *Anima mea* is notated only in *FM*. This manuscript lacks the *faulx bourdon* inscription; this composition has been transcribed in the *Denkmäler der Tonkunst in Oesterreich*, VII p. 174 and in DCS 29.

[3] The following versions, primarily from *Tr 90* & *93*, lack the fauxbourdon inscription: 98. *Em* (W) 210; 99. *Tr 90* 816, *Tr 93* 1627; 102. *Tr 90* 840, *Tr 93* 1652; 105. *Tr 90* 842, *Tr 93* 1655; 107. *Tr 90* 813 *Tr 93* 1624; 109. *Tr 90* 792, *Tr 93* 1598; 111. *Tr 90* 852, *Tr 93* 1664; 112. *Tr 90* 851, *Tr 93* 1663; & 113. *Tr 90* 833, *Tr 93*, 1644.

Title and Composer	Meter & Voices	Em	Trent & Misc.	Ao
104. Gaudeamus, Anonymous	C 2		*90* 841; *93* 1654	
105. Gaudeamus, Sarto	(O) p2 & ¢			11
106. In medio, Anonymous	(O) 2	(W) 213	*92*(I) 1372	
107. Nos autem, Anonymous	¢ p2			15
108. Os iusti, Anonymous	C 4T		*88* 205	
109. Puer natus, Anonymous [1]	O p2	(B) 147	*92*(I) 1365	
110. Resurrexit, Anonymous	¢ p2		*Strahov* f. 22v	
111. Salva sancta, Binchois	(O) p4T&2			2
112. Salva sancta, Brasart	(O) p2			9 [2]
113. Sapientiam, Brasart	(O) p2			14
114. Spiritus Domini, Anonymous	(O) 2		*90* 808; *93* 1619	
115. Spiritus Domini, Sarto	(O) p2 & C		*92*(II) 1522	8
116. Statuit ei, Anonymous	O 2	(W) 212	*92*(I) 1457	

ANTIPHONS

Title and Composer	Meter & Voices	Trent 92 (I)	ModB	Miscellaneous
117. Benedicite Dominum, (Merques)	(O) 2	1485		
118. Crucifixam in carne, Anonymous	(¢) p2			*FM* 38
119. Crucifixam in carne, Anonymous	¢ p2			*FM* 35
120. Cum iocundate, (Merques)	(O) 2	1478a		
121. Da pacem, Binchois [3]	(¢) 2		53	*Em*(W) 175; *Ver 761* 25
122. Hic vir, Dufay	C 2		46	
123. Magne pater, Fede	¢$_3$ 2		42	
124. Nativitas gloriosae, (Merques)	(O) 2	1478		
125. Petrus apostolus, Dufay	C 2 [4]		48	*CS 15* 82

[1] *Tr 90* includes a contratenor which has the same part as the tenor; the fauxbourdon inscription is missing.

[2] For *Tr 90* 851, an alternate fauxbourdon tenor is provided for the introit proper in *Ao* but not in *Tr 90*. The psalm verse and the gloria patri for the cantus and tenor include the *faulx bourdon* inscription in *Ao*. Note! none of the above compositions is available in a modern transcription.

[3] Although no mensuration is given for *Da pacem*, it is written in the same style, rhythmic as well as melodic, as the other antiphons in this section of *ModB* with ¢ or C mensuration. The mensuration, in context, should be duple instead of triple as transcribed by Marix p. 192 and BukofzerPP p. 45.

[4] Only the cantus and tenor are contained in *ModB*. An anonymous altus and bassus in addition to the cantus and tenor are found in *CS 15* as a *A faulx bordon si placet*. *CS 15* makes some changes in Dufay's cantus and (especially) in his tenor.

Title and Composer	Meter & Voices	Trent 92 (1)	ModB	Miscellaneous
126. Propter nimiam, Dufay [1]	Ȼ 2		54	*FM* 44
127. Regali ex progenie, N. Merques	(O) 2	1508		
128. Regina celi, Lymburgia [2]	C&Ø 2			*BL* 199
129. Sancti Dei, Binchois [3]	Ȼ 2		52	
130. Sapiente filio, Dufay	C 2		45	

MASS MOVEMENTS

Title and Composer	Meter & Voices	Printed Transcriptions
131. Kyrie (*Cunctipotens genitor*), Anonymous [4]	(O) p2	
132. Kyrie (*Cunctipotens genitor*), Dufay	(O) p2	BesselerBF p. 19 inc
133. Kyrie (*Fons bonitatis*), Anonymous	O 2	
134. Kyrie (*Jesu* redemptor), Anonymous	(O) p2	
135. Kyrie (*Jesu redemptor*), Brasart	O 2	
136. Kyrie (*Jesu redemptor*), Dufay	O 2	DTÖ Bd. 16 p. 80
137. Kyrie (*Lux et origo*), Anonymous	(O) 2	
138. Kyrie (*Lux et origo*), Roullet	O & Ø 2	
139. Kyrie (*Orbis factor*), Anonymous	(O) 2	
140. Kyrie (*Orbis factor*), Dufay	(O) p4T	BukofzerF p. 42 inc
141. Kyrie (*Pater cuncta*), N. Merques	(O) p2	
142. Kyrie (*Rex Deus aeternae*), Anonymous	(O) p2	
143. Kyrie (*Firmator sancte*), Anonymous	O 2	
144. Kyrie (without any trope), Grossin	O 2	
145. Gloria, Anonymous	O p3b	
146. Gloria, Anonymous	C p2	DTÖ Bd. 61 p. 33
147. Sanctus, Anonymous	(O) 2	
148. Sanctus [5], Dufay	Ø p2	
149. Agnus dei [5], Dufay	Ø p2	
150. Sanctus, R. Liebert	(O) p3s	DTÖ Bd. 53 p. 16
151. Agnus Dei, R. Liebert	(O) 2	DTÖ Bd. 53 p. 17
152. Benedicamus Domino, Anonymous	(O) 2	

[1] Transcribed in BesselerBF p. 264.

[2] Transcribed in BesselerBF p. 18 inc.

[3] Transcribed in Marix p. 218.

[4] In the catalogue of Margareta Melnicki, *Das einstimmige Kyrie des lateinischen Mittelalters*, (Dissertation, Erlangen, 1954), the cantus firmi of the Kyries are as follows: *Cunctipotens genitor*, No. 18; *Fons bonitatis*, No. 48; *Jesu redemptor*, No. 68; *Lux et origo*, No. 39; *Orbis factor*, No. 16; *Pater cuncta*, No. 58; *Rex deus aeterne*, No. 96; and *Firmator sancte*, No. 132. The Kyrie without trope in this source is No. 117.

[5] The fauxbourdon sections of the Sanctus and Agnus are the same except for the final cadence.

SOURCES FOR THE MASS MOVEMENTS

	Em	Trent 92 (I)	Trent 87	Trent 90 & 93	Ao	Miscellaneous
131.		1402 [1]				
132.	(B) 56	1387			20	*BU*62&*BL*(N) 123
133.				*90* 854; *93* 1666		
134.		1373				
135.	(B) 155			*90* 872; *93* 1684	21	
136.	*(W) 214		(I) 67 & 76			
137.	(W) 242					
138.	(W) 196		(I) 73			
139.				*90* 876; *93* 1688		
140.	*(B) 62	1396	(I) 68	**90* 878; **93* 1690	29	
141.		1454				
142.				*90* 879; *93* 1691		
143.				**90* 881; *93* 1693		
144.					51	
145.			(II) 191			
146.			(II) 180			
147.	(W) 223					
148.		(II) 1563				
149.		(II) 1564				
150.	*(B) 137	(I) 1418				
151.	*(B) 138	(I) 1419				
152.	(W) 239					

SEQUENCES

Title and Composer	Meter & Voices	Em	Tr92 I	Tr87 I	Tr93	Tr88
153. Congaudent angelorum, Anonymous	(O) p2				1744	
154. Isti sunt, Dufay	O p2			40		
155. Lauda sion, H. Edelawer	(O) p2	(W)276			1760	
156. Lauda, sion, Dufay	O p2		1452			
157. Laus tibi Christe, Roullet	C p2			43		
158. O beata beatorum, Roullet	O p2			46		
159. Omnes sancti, Roullet	Ͼ p2			45		
160. Sacerdotem Christe, Roullet	O p2			44		
161. Verbum bonum, Edlerawer	(O) 2	(W) 11				
162. Verbum bonum, Anonymous	Ȼ p2					455
163. Verbum caro, Anonymous	(O) 2		1374			

[1] Incomplete; only the cantus and tenor are written for Kyrie I and II, and Christe I and II. Fauxbourdon is contained only in the second Kyrie and Christe. The contratenor is wanting for the Kyrie I and Christe I and all voices for Kyrie III.

MISCELLANEOUS

Title - Composer - Type	Meter & Voices	Published
164. Deus in adiutorium, Anonymous (Versicle and Response)	(C) 2	
165. Et cum spirituo tuo, Anonymous (Preface)	(O) p2	
166. Supremum est, Dufay (Motet)	Ø p2	DufayO Vol. II & DTÖ Bd. 76 p. 24
167. Viderunt omnes, Anonymous (Communio)	Ø 2	
168. Vos qui secuti, Dufay (Communio)	(Ø) 2	DufayO Vol. IV & BesselerUF etc.
169. Iuvenis qui puellam, Dufay (Motet)	₵ p2	WolfGdM, Vol. II & Facs. Vol. III
170. Hic dixit possum, Anonymous (St. Matthew Passion)	C p2	
171. Te Deum... O blesse God, Anonymous (Carol)	(O) p2	Miller p. 62
172. Kyrie... audi nos, Anonymous (Litany, *feria 2*)	(C?) 1	Harrison p. 411 & BukofzerF 31 inc
173. Kyrie... audi nos, Anonymous (Litany, *feria 3*)	(C?) 1	
174. Kyrie... miserere, Anonymous (Litany, *feria 4*)	(C?) 1	Harrison p. 412 inc
175. Terrible dame, Busnois (Chanson)	C p2 [1]	PirroH p. 120 (fb. complete)

[1] The chanson itself is written for four voices, but in the fauxbourdon sections only two voices are used at a time.

SOURCES FOR THE MISCELLANEOUS COMPOSITIONS

BL	Em	ModB/C	Trent	Miscellaneous
164.	(W) 234			
165.	(W) 197a			
166. (N) 168	(W) 219	*B* 68	*92*(I) 1391	*BU* 40
167.	(W) 208			
168. 119			**87*(I) 36	
169.				*MüL* 13
170.		*C*(II) 82		
171.				*Ritson* f. 26^{v}
172.				*LP 438* f. 180^{v}
173.				*LP 438* f. 180^{v}
174.				*LP 438* f. 180^{v}
175.				*Pix* f. 160^{r}